"This book feels like a walk in the woods with an encouraging friend. One of those walks you take after a delicious meal, where you're walking but still carrying your wineglass. As you walk, you open up your heart to really listen, and your friend is brutally honest without being hurtful. And your friend tells you the truth about themselves, which is almost exactly the truth about yourself, and it sets you both free. Jonathan Martin took me on such a walk in *The Road Away from God*. His words, his stories, his journey are a true gift. And even though the book's title might contradict this . . . while reading, I think I found Jesus again. I think you will too."

Carlos A. Rodriguez, founder of The Happy Givers
and author of *Drop the Stones*

"Whether you are among the countless walking wounded who have fled religious institutions for their spiritual lives or have edged slowly away from what was once your sacred home to find yourself in the wilderness, Jonathan is a one-man welcome wagon. He's arrived at your door with a hot dish, a field guide for navigating your new landscape, and a contagious, humble faith in your spirit knowing where it needs to go to find what it needs to find. I am blessed to count Jonathan among my most trusted friends and spiritual companions, and now, dear reader, you can too."

Cathleen Falsani, journalist and author of
Sin Boldly: A Field Guide for Grace

T0051279

"In this timely and well-written book, Jonathan Martin joins us for a long walk on the Emmaus road, which these days is crowded with disappointed and disillusioned people forlornly trudging away from the high hopes they once held for the Christian faith. But Jesus is full of surprises and doesn't give up on any of us—even the most despairing. Martin patiently reminds us of this beautiful truth as he gently whispers how the road away from God can become the road back home. I am grateful for the help and hope this book will bring to so many."

Brian Zahnd, pastor of Word of Life Church and author of *When Everything's on Fire*

"In a sea of deconstruction how-to guides, Jonathan Martin offers something uniquely different. *The Road Away from God* reads less like a map to follow and more like postcards from a seasoned fellow traveler. In each chapter, Jonathan Martin offers his trademark blend of endearing approachability and nurturing pastoral care without ever giving way to the temptation of easy answers with neatly tied bows. In the end, readers will come away with a profoundly changed awareness of the God who has been traveling this road with them all along."

Stephanie Tait, author and disability activist

"There is no one more uniquely qualified to help us navigate the spiritual crisis of our time than Jonathan Martin. His own wounds, scars, and shipwrecks have gifted him with the empathy and tenderness to discern Christ in the chaos. *The Road Away from God* is a timely work, gently reminding us that the God we left behind was limited. And while the desolate, godforsaken road of deconstruction may feel lonely, we are not alone, for it is here that we finally meet the limitless Christ of the cosmos."

William Matthews, recording artist and singer-songwriter

"While reading Jonathan's book there were moments when I felt that he was sharing my personal journey with the world. I felt seen, heard, and held in a warm embrace of words that comforted my soul. It was as if someone was walking next to me on my own road, reminding me that I'm right where I'm supposed to be and Godishere."

Anjelah Johnson-Reyes, comedian, actress, and author

"Jonathan Martin challenges proclaimers of the gospel and secularists alike to take inventory of their practices. His words and ministry demand that our democracy face its myths and reconcile with the truth. Spiritual communities and our civic society are better because of people like Jonathan who have a deep commitment to democracy, artistry, compassion, and reconciliation through Christ's love."

Rev. Dr. Otis Moss III, pastor of Trinity United Church of Christ

THE ROAD AWAY
from GOD

HOW LOVE FINDS US
EVEN AS WE WALK AWAY

JONATHAN MARTIN

BakerBooks

a division of Baker Publishing Group
Grand Rapids, Michigan

Published by Baker Books
a division of Baker Publishing Group
PO Box 6287, Grand Rapids, MI 49516-6287
www.bakerbooks.com

Printed in the United States of America

Library of Congress Cataloging-in-Publication Data
Names: Martin, Jonathan, 1978– author.
Title: The road away from God : how love finds us even as we walk away /
    Jonathan Martin.
Description: Grand Rapids, MI : Baker Books, a division of Baker Publishing
    Group, [2022] | Includes bibliographical references.
Identifiers: LCCN 2021052316 | ISBN 9781540902160 (paperback) | ISBN
    9781493437559 (ebook)
Subjects: LCSH: Spirituality—Christianity. | Non-church-affiliated people. | Faith.
Classification: LCC BV4509.5 .M31155 2022 | DDC 248.4—dc23/eng/20211118
LC record available at https://lccn.loc.gov/2021052316

To protect the privacy of those who have shared their stories with the author, some
details and names have been changed.

The author is represented by the Christopher Ferebee Agency, www.christopher
ferebee.com.

Baker Publishing Group publications use paper produced from sustainable forestry
practices and post-consumer waste whenever possible.

22 23 24 25 26 27 28   7 6 5 4 3 2 1

Contents

1

The Road Called Godforsaken

THERE IS A ROAD called *Godforsaken,* leading from the place you came from and stretching to the place you are now. It's the long road from idealism to hard reality, from innocence to knowing. There was a time when you knew a sacred space, but that sacred space became unsafe long ago. It might have been a building with a steeple, a sanctuary or a temple, or a place that wasn't religious at all but felt sacred to you—a house, a room, a secret hideaway. It could have been any place, anywhere, but it was a place that felt like home, a place where you first came to feel joy, delight, wonder.

But then something happened in that sacred space that broke your trust, and the place that once felt like a dream turned into a crime scene. Maybe it was the ugliness of evangelical politics, the hidden then not-so-hidden hypocrisy of a leader being revealed, or the dissonance between someone worshiping God on Sunday and then posting dehumanizing slogans on Facebook on Monday. The place where you once found faith became the very place where you lost it. You may never feel like you know exactly how to grieve the death of a person or a relationship, but where do you even begin to learn how to mourn the loss of *belief*? Somewhere along the way you became disillusioned with an institution, with an authority figure, or with yourself (at least the self everyone expected you to be), and so you took off walking—not knowing where you were going, only knowing there was no going back to where you came from.

This is more than a metaphor. The road is terribly real, as you know from the hard miles it puts on your mind and body. But at the same time, it doesn't exist on a map. The shape of it, the contours of it, bend in the shape of your heartbreak. The most common, universal experience of the road is that it is long and lonely. And while it clearly seems to lead away from one place, it doesn't seem to lead you any place in particular. In fact, you wonder if it is leading anywhere at all.

If you haven't yet physically left the building, don't let that fool you into thinking you aren't already on the road. If the time has already come when the house is too small for you, when the system and structure no longer work for you, and the beliefs that kept your life purring aren't holding you up anymore, then your soul knows this: you are already out walking.

I have written about shipwreck, but this is not that book again. This is not about failure and loss in general but about the very particular unraveling of belief, the undoing of hope. This is for those disillusioned disciples I talk to every day for whom faith feels less like an anchor for the soul and more like a piece of shrapnel they can't remove. This is for the pastors and church leaders I know who are already bloodied from these deepest questions of the soul, but fear they'd be utterly torn to shreds if they were honest about what they really thought.

Sometimes, as you try to drive far enough into the horizon to forget yourself, the road feels bleak, a long, desolate, forgotten route through the heartland with occasional stops at a no-name motel. Sometimes the road is full of novelty, like an old seaside carnival, with a Ferris wheel, funnel cakes, and mermaids. But even when the road goes from desert into Las Vegas, populated by people and spectacle, the loneliness of feeling exiled from your people never really goes away.

There is a voice in your head that tells you on repeat, "You're on the wrong path," and if you were so brave or so foolish as to ask, there would be more than enough people in your old life to confirm that this road is surely the wrong road. This road is surely the wrong road because it has been so difficult. This road is surely the wrong road because it has felt so lonely. This road is surely the wrong road because you don't know where you're going, and leaving on a trip without a destination surely means you are headed nowhere. This road is surely the wrong road because it's cost you nearly everything you have, and all you have is way too much to pay for a road to nowhere.

Whatever the reason you left, whatever made you do it, whatever got you started, whatever you are walking away from, or whoever you are running away from, this is where you are now. If the reason involved the death of a dream or hope turning to heartbreak or sacred space becoming an unsafe space, I have good news for you: where you are is precisely where you are supposed to be. Perhaps that sounds unreasonable to you, seeing as how you may not know how you feel about matters of God and destiny. You did, after all, pick up a book titled *The Road Away from God*. I don't know all the particulars or complexities of your story. But here's what I do know: contrary to what anybody might be telling you or you might be telling yourself, this is not a detour. You are walking the main artery. Even if you feel like you missed an opportunity somewhere along the way—to take the job, mend the relationship, make the different choice that you think would have made life so much better—that doesn't mean you missed your turn.

Because you've been walking for a long time, and because you've had so many voices in your ear saying that you should have gone this way or that way, please lay down that bag of stones on your back, take a breath, and let this wash over you for a minute. As you will see, self-help clichés and denial are not what I do, so this is not coddling. Dare to believe this might actually be the ground beneath you for a minute, dare to believe this is what's really real:

> You did not make a wrong turn.
>
> You did not miss your turn.
>
> Whatever heartbreak got you here, whatever caused you to question if you screwed up the master plan, know this: you are precisely where you need to be.

If you had only gone this way and not that—well, then you wouldn't be where you are now, with the sweet, throbbing, tender grace of this moment. If you had only known better—well, it's impossible to time travel back to your former self and tag out your former self like a professional wrestler and do it differently. You know what you know now. Or hey, better yet . . . you don't know what you don't know now, which means the world is open to you in this moment and there is now possibility.

No, you are not too old to find yourself in a new narrative. No, it's not too late to find a place or a people where your soul can finally feel at home.

I really don't know how you are going to feel about this, especially if your particular disillusionment with faith or with a faith system has caused you to question the existence of God altogether—which is not only a normal but also often a necessary part of walking this road. But imagine for a moment walking all these miles of dusty, barren road until the vast emptiness fully matches the vast emptiness of your soul. You are fully adjusted to the reality that, at least in a cosmic existential way, you are out here all by yourself. It was your decision to leave on the road called *Godforsaken*; you have walked all this way on your own, and wherever you decide to stop and settle and build something new, you will do that on your own too.

Then in the distance, you see something that looks like a street sign. This is a road without markers, a road you have walked by instinct and intuition, with no maps and no GPS. Wiping the salty sting of your sweat out of your eyes, you wonder if it is a mirage, an illusion, an invention of your imagination. But the closer you get to the dust-covered sign, the more you know you didn't dream this up. The road you've been traveling all this way, the road you called *Godforsaken*, has a name. You take another step in, peering for a closer look. The sign doesn't read *Godforsaken*. It reads *Godsent*. You blink and look again, and it reads *Godinhabited*. You wipe your sweat, blink, look again, and see these words:

Godishere.
Godishere.
Godishere.

If you did in fact miss the exit back somewhere, then God missed the exit too. God, as it turns out, is where you are. And if where you are is where God is, then where you are is right where you're supposed to be.

Leaving the Sacred City

Before anything went sideways—before there was a story about a religion to tell, before there were any stories about priests and preachers, about church councils and doctrines and traveling evangelists—there was a simple human story about two men grieving the excruciating loss of a friend. They weren't trying to start a new religion; they were devout Jews who saw themselves as part of a reform movement within their tradition. They had become students of the Rabbi Jesus, who they believed to be the Messiah, the anointed One, the One who would restore their people to their former glory and help engineer the overthrow of an oppressive Roman imperial regime. Their little homegrown movement was far from the face of an empire. They were under the boot of it—they were brown-skinned, persecuted people.

Jerusalem for them was the holy city, the sacred city, the center of the universe as they knew it—the city that shaped their language and their dreams. But hours before, the sacred city had been the very place where they saw Jesus of Nazareth tortured and killed, mangled and disfigured in front of them. The sacred space was not a safe space for them anymore. The city of dreams had become ground zero for all their nightmares. So they did what a lot of people do when the worst thing happens (well, except of course for the women, as the Gospels draw for us in stark relief): they fled the scene. They got away as quickly as they could from the place that now held nothing for them but trauma.

To walk from Jerusalem toward Emmaus is not just to walk away from the city. It is to walk away from the temple and the God they met in it. It is to walk away from the faith that nurtured them and told them they were part of some larger story that might change the world. To walk away from Jerusalem is to walk away from God—or at least from the God they knew then. Luke 24 is unclear as to the exact reason for their journey. Perhaps they are walking home for the night or for a meal. Whatever logical reason they would have given for their journey, the theological reason is not unclear at all: their hope is dead. They are leaving hope behind and abandoning whatever had ahold of them before. They are walking away.

They are walking on the road from Jerusalem to Emmaus, from certainty into the unknown, from the sacred into a disillusionment that feels profane. Where they are going is less clear than what they are leaving behind. They are walking away from the holy city, away from the temple, away from the God they worshiped in it. They are walking away from the people and the places that had made them. They are walking away from the place where they learned to pray as children, walking away from the One whom Moses met in the center of the flame—walking away with no return address.

The ground that was hallowed to them before is haunted now. The temple at the center of all their hoping and dreaming and worshiping has been desecrated. The holy city itself has been desecrated because it is now known as the place where they watched God die. They saw hope strung up like an animal, bleeding out onto the ground.

It wasn't just their friend who died—Love itself died. Their own life's meaning and their dreams for the future are now swaddled with the limp body of God inside a rented tomb. Their dreams are locked inside death's cellar, the entrance sealed with a rock heavy as grief.

When the hurt is great enough, you don't have to have a particular destination; you just know intuitively you can't go back *there*. And intuition is about all you have when you don't have your teacher or your lover or your home or your old-time religion. You walk, only because it hurts too much to stand still.

And so they walk . . . deeper into disillusionment and despair. They are walking right off the edge of the map of the known world. They wonder if they can walk far enough or long enough to escape the taunting demon of false hope in the rearview mirror.

An Accidental Church

So these two men are out walking down their own lonely road, looking like no one in particular. If you had passed them as the day turned to dusk, you might not have noticed the haunting. From a distance, it's hard to tell the difference between the gait of a person walking to somewhere and the gait of a person walking away from something. These are weathered, working-class men, used to burying any unwanted emotions well behind their eyes. You would have had to walk closer to feel the death that hung heavy in the air between them.

Heartbreak hung between them too, like the man stretched out between two thieves. They are grieving the loss of every dream they ever had—the loss of religion, of tradition, of promise, of yearning. It is as if all their desires bled out with him, so that now all they have is the road ahead of them, all they have is the walking.

To stand still would be to let the horror catch up with them, and that is not an option. When the leather of their shoes starts to rub their feet raw, the sores are a welcome distraction from the harsh rub of reality against their open wounds.

They walk in silence those first few miles because what is there to say, really, while walking away from the city where they watched Love die?

The day grows as heavy as their hearts, the dam breaks, and they finally begin to speak of the unspeakable— they begin to speak of what happened. Tears finally pour forth from these weathered sailors. Torrents of grief upon grief upon grief. The men have lost their appetite for holy things, so there are no pretensions of piety or God-talk. And yet in the simple act of sharing their deepest pain, their sacred grief, something undeniably holy happens between them.

But they are not building altars to any gods here, only to their own grief, only commemorating the holiness of their own pain. They are not talking about the power of God but the spectacle of watching God die. Their ancestor Jacob gathered stones to commemorate his wonder of the Almighty. Why not gather some for their sorrow now, when sorrow is all they have left?

Most who walk the road called *Godforsaken* walk it alone, at least for a little while. But in that moment, the men feel something powerful binding them together, like a hymn binds people together, like stories passed down bind father to son. But this is not heritage or hope holding them close; this is the shared sensation of primal grief. The things they saw and felt, they saw and felt together, the hope and faith they lost, they lost together—as a kind of shared sacrament.

They have no hope for resurrection, only memories in which the dead seem as likely to haunt you as help you. They have no hope at all, only the shared sensation of their hearts having been ripped out. The only thing redemptive about their pain is that it is not solitary; it is shared. It is not the sometimes performative grief of funerals but the savage, unpolished agony only those who have had someone they loved more than life ripped from them can truly know.

There is a kind of grief so bottomless that it, like love and wonder, is transcendent, big enough to get lost in. It's the kind of space that's left when a true believer believes no more. As with making love and speaking in tongues, there are no words for it. There are no prayers to pray and no hymns to sing, only two humans abandoning manners, going all the way into a pain too deep for words, letting themselves get carried away in the cadence of mourning. . . . *Do you remember when this happened? . . . Do you remember how it felt when that happened? . . .*

There is no other word for what was happening between them but . . . *holy, holy, holy.*

So as these two companions walk away from home, they do the only brave and noble thing for no brave or noble reason: out of sheer desperation, they name their searing pain. They do not contain their heartbreak, their rage, or their questions. Faithfulness and fidelity won't sustain them now; honesty is the only remaining virtue. Sorrow gushes from their open mouths like the blood, water, and gore that poured out from Christ's wounded side. They speak the unspeakable to each other on the long, hard road away from God.

This is where the story gets strange, because the story they are telling themselves and each other is not the story God is telling of their lives. More often than not, perhaps, our lives tell a different story than the one we think they tell. As they are walking away from the holy city, away from God, away from God's people, away from their community, as they risk vulnerability and partake of the sour sacrament of shared pain, these two disillusioned disciples are becoming a community. In walking away from the temple, they are becoming a temple—a place in which the Holy of Holies dwells. It takes only two people to make a community possible. You don't have to share piety to have one—in fact, piety is often the biggest obstacle to community. Nobody really bonds over shared piety anyway, but over shared pain.

In a story soon to brim with aching human hilarity, they set out on the road away from God, but their shared brokenness is an invocation to the God they left behind. Vulnerability and shared pain draw the presence of Love, even when they are trying to walk away from it. In the very act of naming their sorrow to each other, in the very act of leaving church behind, they are becoming a church.

> **Nobody really bonds over shared piety but over shared pain.**

Jesus said it long before, but he said a lot of things, and this is no time for remembering his promises or Beatitudes—all the words are running together. But later, in a clearer moment, they will remember: "Where two or three are gathered in my name, I am there among them" (Matt. 18:20). The numbers he named were not accidental. The idea was that "Whenever two are gathered together, I will come and be the third among them."

Two people share the sanctity of grief, and suddenly, a third joins them on the lonely road. Unbeknownst to them . . . God walks with them, unannounced. When you add one person's despair, another person's disillusionment, and mutual empathy, sometimes you create an accidental church, whether you mean to or not. A third man walks along, in the guise of the stranger, and then there are three. Despair, experienced alone, is the deepest and darkest hell. Shared, grief and longing build a holy cathedral, a place for the Spirit to dwell.

But pain also has a way of blinding you to holy things, of keeping you from seeing the inherent holiness not only of the stranger but also of a friend, and the sacredness of the dark path you are walking. So for the time being, these two disciples cannot see God on the journey with them. They cannot see grace or love or mercy walking with them in the valley of the shadow of death.

No matter. Love does not need a permission slip to follow you into the heart of darkness. God doesn't need to be believed in to accompany you where you are going. You can choose whatever path you need to, wherever it might lead you. But you can't choose to walk it alone, no matter how hard you try.

Two disciples set out on the long road away from God. And their story is a microcosm for the stories all our lives must ultimately tell—of how the path of tears, of loss and regret and death, is actually a collision course with resurrection.

Strange Overtones

The men are lost in the sacredness of their shared pain when all of a sudden a stranger walks behind them, breaking the spell. How long has he been there? The road had been empty for miles, untroubled by a single sound save the crunch of the ground beneath their feet. How did they not hear him before? He doesn't look like an intruder, but his presence in their ritual of grief is deeply intrusive, an imposition. The man comes uninvited into the midst of their pain, as if it is their shared vulnerability that drew him there, like a moth to a flame.

The events the two men have been talking about are headline news in their little corner of the world, but this conversation is not political or academic. They are talking about the deepest, rawest, most profoundly personal events of their entire lives. And the stranger, oblivious and open-faced, asks them a seemingly trivial question in light of the weight of their grief: "What's this you're discussing so intently as you walk along?" (Luke 24:17 MSG).

The two men look at each other in the knowing way you do when suffering fools, shooting each other a look that says, *Which one of us is going to have to tell him?* The one named Cleopas breaks the stare first with a bit of a side-eye to look back at the stranger and asks— with as much artificial politeness as he can muster but still unable to veil his incredulity—"Are you the only one in Jerusalem who hasn't heard what's happened during the last few days?" (v. 18 MSG).

And the stranger, in that moment, has a comically goofy face right out of a Monty Python sketch, the New Testament's single greatest account of trolling. The man, whom they do not notice has holes in his hands and his feet and a puncture wound in his side, deadpans and says, "What things?" (v. 19).

23

Exchanging another quick glance between them, the two men still cannot believe the insolence of the stranger, the lack of self-awareness on display as he interrupted such an intense conversation to begin with—much less that the man can somehow live here and have no idea of the bloody events that happened in the last few days that ended the world as they knew it.

But with an ever so slight roll of the eyes and an even less perceptible sigh, they proceed, then, to tell God all about how God has just been tortured and crucified.

What Sent You on the Road?

The story of these two disciples on the road is an extraordinary one, a story that I will contend captures all the major movements of the spiritual life—from the inciting incident that sets us on the path, to the solitary grief that breaks us open so that we have to find a community to learn how to bear it, to the moments of clarity when we actually do see that there is life on the other side of dying, to the bittersweetness of feeling those moments of clarity slip away, to feeling the longing inside that is left in the aftermath. This story is big and broad enough to contain each of our own stories. My hope is that in the pages ahead, you will step into it, come to trust it.

But the object here is not just to tell you a story but to get you to think about the story your life is telling. Whatever you believe about the Emmaus road story in Luke's Gospel, which actually has a lot of room for ambiguity, uncertainty, and unknowing, the movements of the story are relatively clear in a way that life sometimes is not. All of life tells a story, but most of life is not like literature—or film or TV, for that matter. Life isn't plotted so all the movements are linear, telegraphed, obviously related. It's much more chaotic, clumsy, and ambiguous than that. We rarely know what's happening at the time, or really what we are doing or why, much less what anything actually means. But for most people I know who have been on the road, there has been a particular moment when they realized, with some kind of deep knowing, that there was no going back to the world as it was, the world as they knew it before. This was the moment that sent them out walking.

For my friend Tosh, a Black woman who has spent most of her life leading worship in mostly white evangelical spaces, it was the silence of the church in the wake of the murder of George Floyd. It was a revelation to see that in the spaces where she had loved and felt loved, she was not necessarily safe. A shattering came with the realization that the people who celebrated her talent did not take seriously her witness, or the fear that she felt as a Black woman living in small-town, rural Indiana in a racially charged climate. Tosh has not walked away from her faith, but she has had to walk away from some of the spaces that once seemed to nurture it. As she became more open about how she really felt about her own experience of being Black in America, the leaders who loved her singing voice hated the stories she told and branded her and her husband radicals, dissidents, backsliders.

Then there's Nicole, who was in the process of finally coming to terms in therapy with her experiences of sexual assault and abuse that dated back to early childhood. She showed up to a large Methodist church on a Sunday morning for the first time, a church culturally different from the charismatic spaces that marked her, feeling bright and hopeful based on the kind people she met and optimistic about trying a faith community that was unlike the only ones she had known. Halfway through the sermon, the pastor put up a picture on the screen of then Supreme Court nominee Brett Kavanaugh and gave an impassioned defense of him, preaching about how the righteous are falsely accused. Between the lines, she felt her own crushing experiences of past sexual trauma belittled. She grabbed her purse and her kids before the benediction and quickly hurried out the narthex door into a wide, ambivalent Oklahoma sky. She tweeted a line about how alienated she felt due to the experience. Immediately, family and friends labeled her a troublemaker, a malcontent, a complainer, and a pastor-killer.

For many folks I know, January 6, 2021, is a day they have never fully recovered from, a day in which toxic ideas and language about God that had seemed implicit became painfully, terrifyingly explicit. The express use of Christian images and words in the Capitol attack was traumatizing for people who already felt a deep seasickness from watching their religion be hijacked in a way that was not just misguided but vile. That kind of religion was publicly exposed as being not just unlike the Jesus we read about in the Gospels but like the antichrist, corrupt to its very core. The insurrection seemed to be a public climax to a story that had been developing for generations—of a white American evangelicalism that was racist, violent, misogynistic, homophobic, a false religion, and unconcerned about creation and the poor. The rot seemed to be not at the periphery of this movement but at the core, not only ambivalent but also an active enemy of the nonviolent One Christians call Messiah. The cross of Jesus of Nazareth, which is ostensibly the symbol of the prophet of Love who revealed to us the universal truth of death and resurrection, was openly used as a symbol of nationalism, racism, militarism, and white supremacy.

It is one thing to feel awkwardly early to the party, a little misunderstood or a little out of place. It is another thing to cross that line where you know that the people you thought were your people are really not your people, the place you called home is really not your home. It is one thing to have some questions you do not know how to answer. It is another thing to know that you have seen something you cannot unsee and that the world you thought you knew is not a world you know or in which you can be seen or known any longer.

For many of us, those experiences became the start of long, isolated roads—like the landscape of US Route 50 in Nevada, known as the loneliest road in America, or like the soundscape of Bruce Springsteen's bleak *Nebraska* album. Most of us start on this kind of journey not as a pilgrim on some kind of spiritual quest but as an exile who knows nothing more than that the place we left is not a place to which we can return. I never cease to wonder at the ways people are labeled rebels who walk the road of disillusionment and despair not because they hate the people or places they come from but because they love them too deeply to bear the heartbreak and horror of watching them exposed as something less than sanctuaries.

Shaken Loose

I understand how becoming disenchanted with the people and places that have shaped you can lead to bitterness, but the faith spaces that made me still shape the language of my dreams. Flannery O'Connor called the American South "Christ-haunted,"[1] and I suppose that the illusive figure of Jesus of Nazareth will never stop haunting me. Jesus always came to me in the shadow of men I revered as giants, as I come from a long line of long people. One of my grandfathers was a pioneering Pentecostal preacher, six foot four, a voice loud and crackling with the thunder of Mt. Sinai. My other grandfather was also six foot four, a man's man of the Johnny Cash variety, not a preacher but an entrepreneurial small business owner who started a furniture business in rural Asheboro, North Carolina. He was a serious man, not given to frivolity exactly so much, but he had a tender heart—and sometimes would just say the most unintentionally hilarious things. He wasn't a hard or judgmental man, but his religion was strict. The other day I remembered him trying to describe a gentleman he knew was a churchman, but Paw found his faith to be peculiar. There was something about the way he said it: "Well . . . he's some sort of a Christian." It was one of those random lines that just kind of stuck in our family, and we laughed about it over and over.

I think if my Paw were still here, he'd love me as much as ever, but perhaps now he would also describe me as "some sort of a Christian." I'm enough of a mutt now that it's never easy to describe in short just what sort of a Christian I am, or aspire to be. The Catholics taught me how to pray, the Eastern Orthodox taught me the deeper mysteries of the Spirit, the Episcopalians opened my heart up wider to the table of God, and the Methodists taught me how to bridge the world between the wildness and the liturgy. The stand-up comedians taught me the timing I needed to learn how to preach. What's for sure is that I'm still S. D. Martin's grandson and I have some of that Sinai electricity burning hot in me too, for God and other things. I'm definitely still a product of the terror and the wonder, perhaps even have almost too much of a wanderlust to find the glory on whatever mountain glory might still be found.

I'll always be Pentecostal enough to be a sort of accidental mystic, and that has served me well the further I've come to recognize the Spirit in the beauty of liturgy. Given my chaotic mind, showing up at the same place at the same time doing the same thing has largely saved my life. When I was a young preacher, I couldn't have imagined preaching being "led by the Spirit," unless I somehow "came up" with the sermon from start to finish. When I started preaching from the assigned lectionary texts most every Sunday, though, I was shocked by how conspicuously, and consistently, the Holy Ghost seemed to get into the proceedings. The lectionary was like a mix tape, and the Spirit was the DJ, and every time I'd be staggered in some way by how relevant the given text was to whatever was happening in the world that very moment.

This is how one of the moments came for me: It was fall of 2016, two days before the climactic showdown between Donald Trump and Hillary Clinton. The world both inside and outside the church couldn't have felt more tense or more fractured. The storm was already in the pews. I wasn't interested in partisan politics as a kind of team sport, and I'm still not, but I was very aware that all spirituality is political, because spirituality ultimately determines how we actually choose to live in the world. The reality that ran deeper than the personalities was a sense of reckoning around race in America, of people grappling with whether or not they could or would trust the perspective of neighbors who didn't look like them, who didn't see the world through the lens of their own self-interest. To crib language from the apostle Paul, it wasn't just personalities we were coming to terms with but "principalities"—

governing forces in systems and structures in the world that were greater than the sum of their parts, determinative ideas that shaped how we see the world.[2]

I was already a long way from my home state of North Carolina, but I was coming to feel further and further away from the spaces I held sacred. In Tulsa, Oklahoma, where I lived then, the city was still reeling from the unprovoked shooting of a Black man, Terence Crutcher, by a white cop, at the same time that my native city of Charlotte was having riots following its own police shooting. Everything was shaking, not least of all me. And while I am no dime-store prophet, my sense all along about that election cycle was that it was a defining time for the church in North America—a time that would have implications for generations to come.

I grieved all that I was hearing and feeling. Whatever sort of a Christian I was, the house I had grown up in had long ago become too small for me. My Pentecostalism now is a big-tent spirituality, the way I'm convinced it was meant to be. This big tent was always a sacred circus, more suited to being outside in the field than inside the cathedral. It was diverse and colorful, without walls. The Pentecostalism that laid claim on me is a peace church tradition that takes seriously matters of justice and peacemaking. But in the cultural landscape in front of me in the middle of America, it was nowhere to be seen. Our churches were just as nationalistic, as full of fear and fearmongering preachers, as anyone else's. Instead of being a movement for people on the margins, the way Pentecostalism was in the beginning, we were actively scapegoating and demonizing the poor, the refugee, the immigrant. Straight Bible language of justice and mercy was suddenly politically loaded and controversial. Anybody I knew who could discern sensed deep down that we were driving over some kind of cliff together.

I was desperate for a word from God. I didn't need a sermon but to climb the mountain the way my grandfather learned to do it, stay until the power came down, and bring a word from God for the people of God. The lectionary took me to the Old Testament book of Haggai, the minor prophet, and reading it, I found a word that was perhaps not what I was looking for but had just the kind of otherness and particularity that I needed. These were words written at the time when Israel was coming out of seventy years of Babylonian exile, tired and broken by a regime that had actively tried to stamp out their language, their culture, and their religion. The Persians had just conquered the Babylonians, and optimism was high that this could be a new chapter for the chosen people. When Haggai was written, the first handful of exiles were returning from Babylon to Jerusalem, the holy city. They weren't walking away from it but finally back toward it.

Yet what they saw when they returned gutted their newborn hope. The temple was in ruins, worse than they had imagined. As it had been for the disciples on the road to Emmaus, the holy place had been desecrated. These captive sons and daughters, raised on the mythology and the hymnody of the temple in all its glory, returned to a sacred site emptied of its former splendor. After seventy years of exile, there were few Jews remaining who could even remember what the glory of the temple was like, much less knew how to recapture it.

It is within this context that the word of the Lord comes to the prophet Haggai: "My spirit abides among you; do not fear. For thus says the LORD of hosts: Once again, in a little while, I will shake the heavens and the earth and the sea and the dry land; and I will shake all the nations, so that the treasure of all nations shall come, and I will fill this house with splendor, says the LORD of hosts. The silver is mine, and the gold is mine, says the LORD of hosts" (Hag. 2:5–8).

This was not precisely the sort of "word" I had hoped for. People seemed tired and restless, agitated. I was on edge from all the rhetoric as much as anyone else. I desperately wanted a word to bring back from the mountain that told everybody it would be fine, and to calm down, and that things would get easier rather than harder. I was still shaking from all the transition in my own personal life, from leaving home and going through divorce. Even in my immediate world, nothing had ever really stopped shaking. In the midst of so much that was already shaking, I wanted a word that would tell me the shaking would stop.

I'm sure Haggai would have rather delivered a word of stability too, especially to a people who had already endured seventy years of captivity. But instead, there was this more provocative word: to a people who were already shaking, God said, "I will shake all the nations." They would not be exempt from it. They would shake like everyone else, just like all the rest of the nations. And yet the word was that in the shaking that came to all the nations, God would have a particular purpose for his own people: God would shake the nations "so that the treasure of all nations shall come" (v. 7). There was a particular treasure God had buried inside this particular people so deep that, as it is with most treasure, the only way for it to come forth was for it to be shaken out. It was buried treasure that would have to be dislodged, shaken so that it might be shaken loose.

This is the promise that Christian faith offers: not that you will be less likely to get cancer or have a car accident, not that you will be less likely to struggle in any of the noble or humiliating ways that created things struggle, but that there might be some purpose of God to be discerned in the struggle. Which is not to say it will make sense to us or entirely redeem all our suffering in this moment.

Yet this shift in perspective is no small one. I am shaking as much as anyone else. I am subject to the same frailties, calamities, and temptations. I am exempt from nothing that is human. And yet in all that shakes, what might the Lord of hosts be shaking loose? In all that rattles my insides, what treasure buried in these depths might yet bring some beauty to the world?

Keep in mind that anything good God ever did for the sake of Israel was always for the sake of the world.

Election—being chosen by God—was about vocation, not salvation. The people of God were chosen, as they always are, to bring God's light to bear in the nations. Thus, it is not as if God exploits the nations to teach his people "a lesson." It's only that in the same shaking that Israel would feel alongside all her neighbors, all the pain and chaos and ruins, this same calamity would bring out of them shimmering treasure, ancient beauty and yet some unspeakable newness.

Faith does not offer a qualitatively different experience of being human. We are all dealt the same splendid, sorry hand. But it does offer us a different lens through which to see this experience. And as the Emmaus road story will so vividly illustrate, seeing is not just believing. Seeing is everything.

Feeling my own insides shaking as much as anyone else's, I got up to preach that Sunday morning in Tulsa with a word of comforting warning, or peculiar comfort: The shaking is not going to stop; it may have in some ways only just begun. It is shaking not just for us but for all nations. But take heart! The treasure of God **Seeing is not just believing. Seeing is everything.** will be shown forth in us even so. Just not until that treasure is shaken out.

It was not that something fundamentally new or different was happening in the world in 2016. As it was in the days of the prophet, it was an apocalyptic time, a revealing time, a time in which the world that already existed was being revealed for what it had always been, and what it was now. The illuminating and excruciating thing was the way this season was revealing both skeletons in the closet and monsters under the bed— trauma from long ago that had not yet been reckoned with and menacing forces that posed an existential threat to the world even now.

There was a fire within the words of the prophet that burned in me, and I preached about all of it the only way I had been taught and the only way I knew how—with my coattails more or less on fire. The message went over about like you would think it would. Some folks heard it with a kind of relief, with pangs of recognition; others experienced the same words as an ominous, unsettling warning, as an overreaction.

What became startlingly clear was that, whatever reasons people wanted to ascribe for this, whoever they wanted to blame or absolve, sharp divisions were being revealed, both in the world around us and in the world inside of us. For the vulnerable among us, those realities were terrifying. I will never forget that Tuesday night of the election, eating sushi in a restaurant while watching the results trickle in. There was a palpable sea change even in the air that night. The waitress, who had been warm and relaxed, seemed tense and nervous. I asked if she was okay. She said that as the results had become more clear, several of the Mexican guys working in the kitchen had started crying, and even walking out, saying they would not come back to work the next day for fear of how the election results would affect their legal status.

The following Sunday I was speaking at a church in Houston that was richly diverse, culturally. I had no other words to offer for the moment but what I had come to see in Haggai about the shaking, so I poured out my heart on the text again. Between services, greeting people and signing books, I was moved and unnerved by the number of people of color who told me that just in that week alone, they had some kind of demonstrative experience with a white person who seemed to feel suddenly empowered to unleash whatever latent feelings of hostility and resentment they had been repressing. A Black woman in her forties told me that a man threw a cup at her and used a racial slur while she was in line at Starbucks. I heard comparably disturbing stories from Asian Americans and Latinos that day.

It can seem impossible that people can live in such close proximity to us and yet experience reality so differently. In Jesus's parable of the rich man and Lazarus, a beggar experiences the comfort and bliss of being in Abraham's bosom, while the rich man begs the man he once ignored to bring him water to quench his thirst while he is being tormented by flames in Hades. The two men are close enough to see and hear each other, so however deep or wide the chasm is between them, the geography that separates them is not great. It is a parable of the afterlife, but the way it actually functions in the text is to illumine the great divide between us: how some people experience heaven and others experience hell within a city block of each other. It is ultimately less a story about the world to come than a challenge to how we live in the world that is: Will we believe the account of our neighbor who experiences life differently than we do, even from a few feet away?

For those who are deluded by false comforts of wealth and influence, the world may still feel like a paradise. But for those who have been on the underside of this reality, recent years have been a time of searing revelation. Some among us have realized that a world that builds artificial paradises, like model homes, across the street from present-day suffering, is no paradise at all—and the unease of this revelation has set them out on a different path from any they have walked before, a road of doubt, questioning, unlearning, and discovery. If you have been unsettled by the reality that what was once handed to you as tidy truth is not true, then the Emmaus road is the road you can and must walk—and likely already are.

2

God on the Road Away from God

I'VE SPENT A LOT OF TIME on the road, talking to people about their journeys both into and away from faith. So much of my own life has been a pilgrimage, heading toward the church house steeple, always in pursuit of the tongues of fire, looking for God and looking to outrun the devil, like a lot of young people on a religious quest. My singular devotion sometimes looked more like an ongoing anxiety attack. Since I was always headed toward the sacred city, it took me a while to become aware of just how many people are on the road going the opposite direction.

Not that my own idealism has been noble. Playing basketball in middle school, I used to try to confess any potential sinful thoughts or motivations that might have occurred between the first and second free throws, convinced that if I didn't keep my heart and mind pure, God would sabotage me by not allowing me to hit the next free throw. I would unplug my Nintendo toward the end of an especially great game of Double Dribble to prove I didn't love it more than God. It was a life of constant examination and fear. As it is for most people, that sort of rigid devotional intensity was not sustainable. Living some real life, not being great at relationships, getting hurt and unintentionally doing some hurting made me much more aware of all the people who weren't manically trying to climb some holy hill, and that manic piety is not perhaps the best frame of living.

The stories of my friends broke me open to the broader cycles, seasons, and rhythms of how larger culture relates to faith. I hear all the time now from people who are, like those two disciples on the Emmaus road, ostensibly walking away from church and away from faith, especially in my Western context. I know that's a larger cultural phenomenon too, but I don't experience this as data on a spreadsheet. I hear it everywhere I go, in coffee shops and text messages and tweets—people who are disillusioned with their faith and the so-called faithful, children of the church who simply feel that the house they grew up in has become too small for them.

The reasons are legion, the usual suspects. They felt let down by their church community or a church leader in some deeply personal way. A science quandary or their own sexuality or a friend's sexuality cracked them open to a world beyond the flat one that was drawn for them. If the faith system they were given proves to be racist or misogynistic or unconcerned with creation or the poor, they aren't wrong to leave it. Some didn't feel like the church they knew in the past could understand or support them on the roads they must go on in the future. Or they just got bored.

So they did the only thing that under the circumstances seemed right—they went walking. They went walking without knowing where they were going or where they needed to go—only knowing that the place where they once felt at home could not be home for them any longer. Even if you don't know the destination, much less how to get there, you can have plenty of perfectly good reasons to know you can't stay in the place that you've been. Sometimes for vocational reasons or out of familial or social pressure, people haven't left the building, but their hearts checked out a long time ago—and they've been walking the road for years without ever leaving the city limits. I don't think there is a more solitary, lonely feeling than that.

I enter into these conversations as a guy who, at this point, is very convinced that God can be seen only from the underside. I'm afraid I am terribly, irrevocably into Jesus. I'm not a fundamentalist, do not pretend to be, am not trying to be. I don't believe in the kinds of wisdom that come from the head of the table, even when I have been at the head of the table. I don't believe in moralism, rationalism, or nationalism. I do believe in joy, wonder, longing. I believe in tenderness. I believe in communities where people can share the joy of common embarrassment without fear. I believe in trusting what you can know on the other side of pain. I believe in resurrection, but only because I tasted it, because the story has carried me along, not because a committee told me I had to. I believe in the Spirit because I feel something holding all things together. I believe in believing some things based on what I feel because experience *is* a way of knowing, which I know because I'm Pentecostal—but not the kind people often want me to be. I don't believe in coercion; I believe in happening. I don't believe in climbing; I believe in falling—because most lessons I have learned about the spiritual life I have learned from the underside of things, not from being on top. Somehow I still believe in the church—but it's complicated, as you will see, because I am complicated, like we all are.

I don't believe in climbing; I believe in falling—because most lessons I have learned about the spiritual life I have learned from the underside of things, not from being on top.

But I am also a believer in walking this road and following the road wherever it takes you. The fact that not everyone who walks will find their way back to some version of religious faith is not a fear that would make me want to keep anyone from walking it. I've been around long enough to know that people will give many reasons, most of them ostensibly good, for why you should never leave your "Jerusalem," your holy place: because it's safer to stick to the people and places you come from, because of loyalty and legacy and continuity and tradition, because of the story of your family and of your people, because you never know what's really on the other side of the walls out there, because we want to protect you from self-destructive choices, and, well, just because . . . just because I said so. If there are good reasons not to walk the road your soul feels it must, I would not know how to articulate them. And if it is disillusionment that sends you packing, I can't imagine that any version of telling you "not all Christians are like that" would change your mind. So I have no interest in doing any of that.

I am not on the board of the Department of Tourism and Commerce for anybody's version of Jerusalem, or whatever place you look to as your spiritual home. I have no vested interest in keeping you in Atlanta or Oklahoma City or Cleveland, Rome or Constantinople. Nor am I interested in getting you to relocate from one to another, though I probably really do think we would all be happier if we lived in New Orleans—with the best food and music in the world.

It is dangerous to dictate other people's spiritual journeys, and good spiritual elders and wise spiritual teachers—let me state this slowly and clearly—absolutely will not do this. Wise guides understand that human freedom is central to every story of faith, that autonomy cannot be run over. I am suspect of any spiritual leader who tells people, "Don't listen to yourself; listen to me." Not because I don't think the "self" is sometimes unwise, addicted, self-destructive, or otherwise misguided but because (1) that language inevitably becomes an exercise in toxic control over someone else's life, (2) I don't think that's what God is like, and (3) that entails a poor understanding of what it is to truly listen to one's "self."

God is not about coercion but freedom. Jesus's story of the prodigal son in Luke 15 illustrates this beautifully. It is a story about a son being given his inheritance early, even though the father knows it will be misspent. He does this because there is something essential about being able to go on a self-directed journey, even if it means coming to the end of one's self. Note how at the end of the story, the prodigal son has a kind of awakening and clarity from walking his road that his elder brother never comes to. God does not control us in any way!

In the deepest and truest sense of the word, we must learn to listen to our "selves": the true self, not the false self, uncluttered by the noise and debris of that which is not good, that which is not love, that which is not light. There is a self worth listening to, a you that does in fact know how to listen to God and discern what is good and right and best for your life—a version of you that can be trusted. As anyone who has been through recovery knows, sometimes it can take a while to get to that version of the self, but even when it is buried under the rubble, it is there, still shining, still gleaming, still blessed.

This is a story about how two disillusioned men come to see. You already know something now that the two disciples do not know, early on the road: that God is already walking with them. And I hope that as you read about them, the story reads you—and you have your own experience of coming to recognize God, to see God, or to come to see something about your way of seeing! And this is the thing that is crucial: it absolutely has to be your own revelation, your own deepest knowing, your own heart's true seeing. There are some things that cannot be taught to us, only revealed, and they can't be revealed to us in any classroom—and this from a person who loves and believes in classrooms. This is the kind of revelation that comes only on this road, on the road away from God. It is a difficult road to walk, and no doubt you have already been tempted to turn around and walk back. Why haven't you?

There is a self worth listening to, a you that does in fact know how to listen to God and discern what is good and right and best for your life—a version of you that can be trusted.

Because, quite simply, you know you cannot stop until you see everything that you need to see, hear everything that you need to hear. You can't stop walking because you aren't done with the road, and the road isn't done with you. You can't stop walking until you find what you went looking for, and even if you don't know precisely what you went looking for, you'll know it when you see it. There may be a time and a way to go back toward the Jerusalem that you came from—there usually is, and we will get to that. But if and when you ever do go back, you will not go back the same way, as the same person, or for the same reasons.

I will tell you some things I have seen along the road I've been walking, but I cannot impose my journey onto yours, because nothing can change the fact that you are out walking what is intended to be your own revelatory road. You didn't stumble onto it. You didn't spill onto it. On some level, you were sent, nudged, pushed. There was something drawing you to this path, drawing you toward something you needed to see. Some part of you knows that. Trust it. Trust the road that so far has led nowhere. Because it actually is going *somewhere*—some part of you knows that too.

I really do believe in the story of the Emmaus road. I believe in the *path* of the Emmaus road. I believe it contains every story. It is the story of Adam and Eve leaving the garden, and of the prodigal son leaving home and going back again. It is the story of a pregnant runaway and heartbroken survivors.

It is the story of how spaces that you once held sacred can be desecrated and haunted.

It is the story of leaving home for any and all kinds of reasons—and of the God who meets you on the road when you do.

It is the story not of losing faith, exactly, but of trading in the one you had before for the one you need now.

It is the story of following the trail of your own heart's deep questions and your own soul's deep lament only to find God walking alongside you, unannounced.

For disciples who have seen too much, heard too much, known too much, it is the only road left to take.

I have officially resigned from our local sacred city Department of Tourism and Commerce. I have no interest in being on God's PR team, convincing anybody why they should not walk away from the world that they've known. I am personally convinced that the Jesus a lot of people are walking away from is not Jesus at all, as the only Jesus I recognize now is an oppressed, persecuted, brown-skinned man who was trampled by an empire, not a mascot who was invented for one. But nothing about what you see on your road can be dictated, for this is very much your path, and the path must be trusted, and you must be trusted to walk it.

I say these things not because I have some blind belief in human progress or to underwrite a vaguely romantic notion of "following your heart," the way we use that phrase in a rom-com. My reasons have nothing to do with your capacity to find meaning—because I can't even find my keys—and everything to do with the One who still walks these haunted roads, who still appears to disillusioned disciples, revealing the mysteries to those who keep walking.

Where Is God on the Road You Are Walking Now?

I know there are people who have questioned the journey you are on and your reasons for setting out on it. I am not one of them. I believe in the road you are walking, even and perhaps especially when the road you are walking is the road away from God. And I believe in the One who walks with you, possibly in disguise.

I have no interest in pointing you back to anything in your past in order to get you to discover some kind of truth. If there is truth to be found, it is to be found right here, right now, hiding in plain sight, in this moment.

Whether you believe it or not, I absolutely do believe that God walks with you here, now. The only question is how? In what form? You need no lecture from me or anybody else about the dangers of leaving where you came from or the dangers of taking the wrong road. You don't need to be berated for being on the "wrong path." You need to be able to recognize God on the path that you're on. And the truth is God walks with you, even on the road away from God.

Make no mistake: God was present with you in the naive safety you had in the place that you came from. But God was also present in the restlessness that stirred you to leave, and he is present with you in the wild now.

I would pray for a miracle, if I thought that's what you needed—for some wild interruption of grace. But the only grace you may need is the grace that has already been given to you—found through eyes that are finally opened.

It is not an intervention you need, only the grace of recognition. And that is what I hope this book, if anything, gives you: not a new road but a new lens through which to see the one you're on already.

What Do You Want?

Some years ago, I was struggling when I was in a place of discernment, and a friend spoke something into me I will never forget. I was wondering, *Should I maybe move to Los Angeles, or maybe to Nashville, or maybe to the city I dream in, the city of New Orleans?* I was in Christa's neck of the woods to speak in Nashville, and Pentecostal mystic that I am, I was ready for any word my highly intuitive friend might speak—really just ready to be told what to do. So I'll never forget what she said when I sat down across from her in a cozy spot in the Urban Cowboy in Nashville. "I have a word for you, Jonathan," she said. "God says, 'I'm not going to give you a word, because I want you to do what you want.'"

Well, that was not the word I was expecting because I tended to assume that what I would want would be of no interest to God, may even be contra the purposes of God. It also would entail the further work of actually excavating what I actually wanted! But something began to click in me then, how sometimes the decision you make is the right decision simply because it's the one you make. It was very much like Christa, as a wise guide, to push me to listen deeper to my own discernment when I came to her like a baby bird, willing to eat anything she would feed me, practically begging to be steered, guided, and controlled. I stress again—*this is what all wise guides do.*

So a week later I was just outside New Orleans, one of the cities I love most, speaking to a little community in Covington. And that night I shared the story of my encounter with Christa and how in this season in which I was longing for a sense of belonging, of home, I was coming to find the home inside, where God is. I talked about what Christa said, about God saying there was no word because God wanted me to do what I wanted. At dinner that night, a friend told me that I should listen to a podcast my friend Rob had done about a similar topic. So as I was making the drive across the bridge to NOLA that night, I leisurely put it on.

I am not one to get things the first time. What I listened to that night was all about how God speaks through our deepest desires—about how when we get through the clutter of the top layer of our superficial wants, our truest desires can be trusted. And with the windows down, feeling that swampy air, seeing the New Orleans skyline at night as I heard the lulling sound of the cars whirring on the bridge, I broke. I think it was the first time that I really believed it, that I really fathomed it. I actually said it out loud into the night as the tears rolled down: "Wow, you actually were serious about this thing I want, weren't you?"

I was happy and incredulous. That wasn't my idea of what God looked like, of what life looked like, of what the universe looked like—that what I want matters, that somehow I have a say in what I will or will not do and what will or will not bring me joy. It was an unexpected, beyond-my-reckoning, where-did-this-come-from, I-can-feel-this-in-my-teeth-and-behind-my-eyeballs kind of joy that took me by utter surprise in the bluesy spring heat. Now I'd just say, that's what resurrection feels like.

As you walk this road in all its ambiguity, is this a question you have even dared to ask yourself: What do I want? Maybe not, or maybe not yet, but dare to now.

What do you want? is a question God asks you on the road as God looks you in the eye. Because your wants are worthy, if you can believe it.

Is it the kind of belonging you feel like you lost? Is it freedom from control and manipulation? Is it companionship, kinship, community? Is it to know that God sees you as beloved? Is it kindness, purpose, clarity?

I don't believe in going on this kind of journey alone. I do believe in community, even when that community is just two or three. And I believe in the power of shared stories passed down through the wisdom and shared practices of a community. I most certainly believe in (and need) wise guides. In fact, I have an absolute embarrassment of riches of those in my life, feel spoiled rotten in that way, and will introduce you to some of them. But I cannot stress strongly enough just how crucial it is, on your own Emmaus road, that you allow yourself to fully embrace the journey in such a way that you are able to see what *you see*, to hear what *you hear*.

Hyperindividuality in our digital age is a real problem, and we often lack the resources to enter into a larger shared story, so perhaps there is a danger in overstating the case. But my sense is that even with all our individuality, we are so tethered to our devices that we spend a lot more time watching someone else's journey than walking our own, to the point where it may be even more difficult to find the kind of differentiation that only the road can give us, where we find the sound of Love and of our own souls for ourselves.

Yet by asking ourselves honestly what *we* want, we can learn to start listening to and trusting our true selves again. As it happens, this is often where we encounter the Spirit as well.

If You Read No Further

I live in relative paranoia thinking about the person who might put this book down early, because there are all kinds of more than acceptable reasons to put a book down early—like getting busy, getting bored, or simply having better things to do. If you are going to put the book down right now, I want to make sure that you remember this: since God is already walking the road with you, you have everything you need to find God on the road you're on. *Pay attention.* Right here, right now, you have everything you need to listen to your life, to hear the whisper of the Spirit on the wind, to know the One who calls your true name, to drown out all the other voices. So the invitation is to practice paying attention.

Books can be good companions on a journey, but they can also be very one-sided conversations, and the last thing you need is a sermon, a monologue. The disciples were not having a one-way conversation when they shared their deepest grief. So I wish I could hear you tell all about it—about how the church broke your heart, or your catastrophic failure, or the doubt that has simmered just beneath the surface for as long as you can remember. Over coffee or a strong drink, if that's what such a conversation would demand, I'd love to hear all your reasons for breaking up with God. It would be okay to talk about the place you lost your true love or to show me the picture of the one who died. You could speak your private doubt. You could say it however you wanted, for as long as you wanted.

Since God is already walking the road with you, you have everything you need to find God on the road you're on.

As the waitress poured us another drink, you could tell me about where and how you got hurt. I promise you there'd be no hint of judgment in these weary eyes. I would be sorry for all that is broken and all that broke you. I would be sorry that faith for you now is such a tired and tattered thing. I know my heart would break underneath the weight of so much pain. My own faith might well have snapped, like a fragile twig, long before yours did. I would not laugh at you or at any of the pain that terrorizes you on the night road that you are now walking.

But if you did see just a teeny bit of laughter in the crinkles around my eyes or sensed just a teeny bit of comedy in the midst of such heavy talk, I'm not laughing at you or at your story. What makes me break a smile is the Love that walks the long night road with you, the clandestine God hiding amid your sorrow, how he will take you by surprise, how he will come not just with tenderness but with such playful mischief, maybe the greatest marker of his presence.

So no, I don't want to lecture you on why you ought to believe or how you ought to change. I don't want to come to God's defense like a low-rent lawyer. I won't try to argue that you cannot or must not leave the house that feels too small for you now.

It's not that I would not worry about you walking any dark roads alone. It's just that—I must say it again—I know that no matter what road you take . . . you'll never be alone on it, no matter how hard you try.

So I want to tell you this, with great respect for whatever story you think your life is telling, whatever story you think your life is telling others, whatever story you think your life is telling even your own self: nobody else gets to decide what your story means. You have plenty of jurisdiction over where you go and what you do and who you become. But what if God is telling a better story about your life than the story you think your life is telling, or the story you tell yourself about yourself?

However bleak your life is, however full of regret or loss or ambiguity, grace is telling a different story about your life than any story you'd dare to tell. There is some relentless beauty taking the fragments of your life and turning them into some textured, nuanced, sprawling story. Grace is telling a story about you, and it would be better if you cooperated. But whether you grant permission or you don't, grace will tell it even so.

The disciples on the Emmaus road see themselves as walking away from faith. Little do they know that simply by walking the natural course of their grief, they are walking a road of inevitability toward resurrection. They don't know that, but they don't need to. The old world is unraveling for them, opening them up for the surprise of the One who makes all things new.

3

When the Story Gets Too Small

ON SOME LEVEL, we are all trying to find our way home—which is no easy proposition when we spend so much of our lives to begin with trying to figure out precisely what and exactly where home is. It is speculated that the two disciples may have lived in Emmaus and that they were actually walking back to their houses in despair. But there is a very different way that they will come to be "at home" with Jesus on the road, a way that calls into question the very nature of what it is to be home: Is home a place that you go to or a place that is in you?

Most every day of my life, I am in conversation with somebody experiencing some level of crisis around whether to go from or stay in a place they once felt they belonged—a faith community, a tradition, an institution. Our sense of where and how we connect to people and places often shifts, and there is no universal, one-size-fits-all answer to the question of whether to stay or go. There is often a faithful way both to stay and to leave, and knowing when and how to do the former or the latter is both tenuous and highly particular.

The only certainty is that you don't need another human to give you permission to go on the journey you have to take. The God who told Abraham to "go from your country and your kindred and your father's house" (Gen. 12:1) is the God of the exodus who is always on the move and who promises to go with you *wherever you go*. So whether or not anybody else gives you permission, God does. Thus, it's never really a question of if you *can* go but whether you have the grace to come or go *now*.

Home . . . Until It Isn't

A faith community or a tradition you grew up in can feel like "home," a place where you belong, until the day it doesn't. Inevitably, we come to moments when the story that held us up before may be what is holding us back from where we must go now. It doesn't mean that the places we have been or the people we have been with are bad or that we were even misguided to live within the more narrow confines of the world we once knew. Those stories and experiences that got us from one place to the next are vitally important; they are often not so much wrong as they are incomplete. I prefer to recognize and affirm the ways that certain structures in my life have served the purpose of carrying me from one place to the next, even when I know they cannot carry me any further. That said, I have had some fairly harrowing experiences of feeling confined, when walls that once held me in and made me feel safe turned into a tomb, so that I felt as if I was being buried alive. And I'm sure you've experienced the same.

When I was young, I worked for a church that at one point had been a source of deep nurture in my life. The pastor was the first person I had ever heard speak vulnerably from the pulpit, and his moments of staggering humanity and healthy transparency have marked my entire life. In the very strict conservative ethos of the churches I grew up in, this was actually the place that largely introduced me to the scandal of grace. I will forever be grateful for those experiences.

But in the years I worked there, the church took a hard right turn on social and cultural issues. The messaging from the stage became harsher, angrier. People in leadership became increasingly eager to prove their own zeal for moral purity codes. I had already been well along the journey of coming to see God, people, and certainly the table of Christ in a more open way, but this was the first time I recall thinking, *If people here knew what I really believe and how I really feel, they would eat me alive.*

We had a bit of a debacle in which one of the pastors on staff wrote a letter to two local ministries that cared for the homeless, telling them we could no longer support them because (1) they also partnered with Catholics, and we could not in good conscience work with people who believed in "works-based righteousness," and (2) one of them had allowed two Muslim college students to work in their soup kitchen. The directors of said ministries were none too pleased with either the significant loss in funding or, I imagine, the gall that anyone would actually write such a thing down. So the story wound up on the front page of the local paper—which is how I and the other staff found out about all of it for the first time.

I cried when I read it. My theology had already broadened and changed so much; I was horrified and embarrassed by our church's stand. I went to the gym to blow off steam and clear my head, and a song that was already a favorite U2 track and one of my shuffle songs came on. The song is "Beautiful Day," and it is all about losing your life to find it: "Sky falls, you feel like it's a beautiful day." I wept on the elliptical machine, feeling this deep confirmation that whatever end I was coming to on this part of my journey was going to be the beginning of everything else.

Then, out of the bazillion songs that could have come next, so help me a live version of the same track came on at random after the studio cut—which had me sobbing and surely had everybody else in the gym questioning my sanity. I am aware of how trivial and banal it might sound to believe that the Spirit can get into the algorithm of an iPod or care about song selection, but I do—which is why I am still weirdly Pentecostal in addition to being "some sort of a Christian."

I was prepared for anything when I got to church the next Sunday, especially since the story had caught on via local news. But my pastor at the time preached a message in which he not only took responsibility for the letter, though he had not penned it, but also talked about how he had forgotten that "you can't bind up the brokenhearted with boxing gloves or wipe tears with the barrel of a gun." He talked about how the church needed a "fresh baptism of love." You may not be past how ridiculous the letter was to begin with, but in the world I was still living in, that apology felt like an extraordinary thing. I hoped maybe it meant we could be backing off the ledge from such exclusionary ideology, but deep down I knew something inside had clicked when I heard that song the way I did. Something was coming to an end to make room for something new.

The whole situation distressed me, but I was still very much at a stage where I felt like I should honor my elders and not make a fuss. So I was quieter than people who know me now would believe I could be. Three months later, the pastor on staff who had written the letter was in a big way of preaching on a Sunday night and went back in harder. He said, "What I said months ago was right. Roman Catholicism is the biggest cult in the world." He went on an absolute tear about how people better not think he forgot which staff and elders didn't stand with him in that little dustup and how he would "no longer sign paychecks for people to stab me in the back."

The worst part was the finale, in which he ended his public shaming of the entire staff with a bizarre reverse altar call of sorts. He called the staff to come and join him on the stage "if you are with me, and I mean WITH ME. If not, go pack up your stuff and don't bother to come back to work tomorrow morning." I was doing student ministry at the time, and I remember sitting in the balcony that night with acid churning in my stomach, literally in a cold sweat. I was young, and as a product of a certain honor culture, I was sure I hadn't said or done anything that made that tirade directed at me. I also knew that not only was I not on board, but that what I was listening to was the most unintelligible, bullying thing I had ever heard in the pulpit, and I was decisively not "with" any of it. I also felt at the time that until or unless I left the church, I was under a certain obligation to be "with" my pastor generally and that what I did or did not do in that moment would affect the students I served there.

It was a very long and public walk down the side steps from the balcony to the stage. I walked it. I hoped it was the right thing. Just now thinking of it, I can still feel what I felt that night in my cells, and it is still honestly one of the worst things I have ever felt. Miraculously, doors opened months after that so that I could depart in a way that felt good and right and peaceful. I made plenty of other significant blunders, but I think somewhere deep down I made a promise to myself never to fold in a moment like that again.

So later on down the road, I got some do-overs. When a spiritual leader in my life told me years later I had to either stop talking about race and justice or walk away from a job that mattered to me at the time, I had to walk away.

There's a bitter irony in religious people acting as if being loving to those unlike them is somehow "selling out" to the world. You can lose your shirt, and they say you did it to get more clothes. You can lose your inheritance, and they say you did it for the money. You can lose your reputation, and they say you did it to become more popular. When I had opportunities later for ministry positions in which I would have had to play down or be dishonest about what I good and well know to be God's unconditional love for my LGBTQ friends, I knew I could not flinch again.

None of these are heroic examples. I had simply changed enough in my life to where there was literally no choice but to be true to what was actually in me or to feel as if I would spontaneously combust. The thing is that at every single one of those turns, I didn't know what refusing to stay in those spaces that had become too small was going to mean, but I knew I couldn't stay in them even so. Leaving always felt scary at first, especially when there were social consequences involved—when being true to what the Spirit was stirring internally would mean being labeled and ostracized externally. But "the truth will make you free" (John 8:32), and actually every step toward what you know to be true is a step toward freedom.

Should You Stay or Go?

The story on which all of Scripture hinges is when God calls a man named Abraham and tells him to "go from your country and your kindred and your father's house" (Gen. 12:1). The wisdom woven almost universally into nearly all wisdom traditions is that a boy must be sent to face the dangers of the wild alone as part of the rite of initiation into manhood. The plotline of every epic and every hero's tale is that a young woman or a young man is either dislodged by force or consciously chooses to leave home to carve out their own journey.

It is even the story of Jesus when he was twelve years old. After attending the festival of the Passover with his parents in Jerusalem, Jesus does not return home with them without saying a word to them about it. He is a good Jewish boy, taught to honor his father and mother—note, he is also "without sin," according to the text.[1] So was this an intentional act of disrespect? When his mother and father realize he is not traveling with their company, they are terrified. They go back to Jerusalem and find him after three days of scouring—"sitting among the teachers, listening to them and asking them questions" (Luke 2:46). His mother is hurt, wounded: "Child, why have you treated us like this? Look, your father and I have been searching for you in great anxiety" (v. 48). Jesus answers, "Why were you searching for me? Did you not know that I must be in my Father's house?" (v. 49). Jesus had to leave one house in order to begin the journey of finding his true home, coming into his larger sense of mission and purpose in the world. He had to leave one version of home in order to find another. There is no path toward home that doesn't entail, as it did for Abraham, leaving the house of your father.

The journey is not about rejecting anything that comes before. Jesus was not rejecting his parents or their tradition. Rather, there was no way that the story of their God would become his story unless he left the place in which he had learned it. That doesn't mean that Jerusalem, the holy place, was now precisely his "home" either.

> **There is no path toward home that doesn't entail, as it did for Abraham, leaving the house of your father.**

This is a central question in the Gospel stories and in each of our own: Where is home precisely? How do we live between "homes"? And if we aren't home yet, how will we know when we get there?

After the conversation with his mother, Jesus goes with them back home—for a long time, apparently twenty years or so—before he eventually goes back to Jerusalem to accept the fate he anticipated even as a child. This was not mere servile acquiescence to his parents' demands. This was a conscious act of surrender. In the process of coming into our own, spiritually and emotionally, it makes all the difference in the world whether or not we know what we are doing and why. Sometimes we may feel compelled to make a decision that feels sacrificial at the time, but that kind of intentional surrender is not the same thing as choosing out of fear or feeling there is not a real choice to make to begin with. Surrender as an intentional spiritual practice is different from merely doing what we are told, because our sense of agency is left intact.

Thus, for Jesus, there was apparently wisdom both in leaving home and in staying home—as will be the case for us at various points in our lives. When it comes to the question of leaving or staying home, timing and discernment are everything, as this narrative shows us. Going home when we may not precisely wish to and leaving when we may not precisely want to can both be acts of faithfulness. There is, evidently, a right way to go and a right way to leave. There is not a universal answer to the question of what we should do. It very much depends on where we are in the journey.

An established sense of home as place was elusive for Jesus, who said, "Foxes have holes, and birds of the air have nests; but the Son of Man has nowhere to lay his head" (Luke 9:58). You are not alone in feeling out of place, hungry for home and belonging. Whatever

other places Jesus found to be places of rest or welcome in the world, Jerusalem, his religious "home,"
would not always be kind to him. He would go back to
his religious home in Jerusalem to clean house at the
temple, driving out the people who exploited the poor
in the name of God. His reli-
gious home would also later be
a crime scene, where he would
be not only criticized and persecuted but also, finally and
ultimately, rejected, tortured,
and killed.

Going home when we may not precisely wish to and leaving when we may not precisely want to can both be acts of faithfulness.

The scene is one of wonder
and delight in which we see
the boy Jesus astonishing the
crowds at the temple, who find
him . . . fascinating in a trick pony kind of way. People
found the boy Jesus "cute," until they recognized a
power in him that felt threatening to their own. Even
a child who was once loved can be seen as an enemy
within their own community. Some of us have had this
experience, of having elders care for us, and maybe
even appreciate and cultivate our gifts, as long as we
were seen as too small to pose a challenge to them. But
when we develop a sense of agency or autonomy, develop a stronger sense of self, begin asking questions,
or simply start finding our voice in a more mature way,
sometimes we find that the memory of a cute child or
a shared history is not nearly as strong as an ego that
now feels threatened.

Is it possible to return to your hometown if you become a different person than you were before you left it—or for that matter, if your hometown turns on you? As we will see later, the story of the two disciples leaving the sacred city in disillusionment and despair does end with a return to Jerusalem. But the journey raises complex questions, for them and for us, of where home really is. It also offers perspective on the age-old question: Once you've made the choice to go walking, *can you really go home again?*

For those of us who are wrestling with such questions, within both the stories of Jesus and the stories Jesus tells, we are given a shocking gift that many of us did not receive within the religious communities we came from: permission to go on the journey. We might think of a strong religious figure as being dominant and controlling, telling us what to do and what not to do, often with the threat of torment just underneath. Curiously, this is not what we see in the Gospels. Jesus often turns the language of judgment against those who use it in an abusive or exclusionary way, as a way of turning the tables. But he doesn't use it to intimidate or coerce people from going on a necessary journey of learning the things that can be learned only on the road, or to coerce people who don't believe into believing.

In fact, in Jesus's famous parable of the prodigal son, which reveals something crucial about the character of God—an answer to the question What is God like?—Jesus gives us an image that is quite opposite of this.

When the rebellious younger son asks the father for his inheritance early—a profound act of disrespect—rather than giving him a lecture or trying to keep him at home, the father gives him the gift wise people always give us: permission to learn for ourselves. He gives him the keys to the family car, knowing his son will make unwise choices—precisely because that is how valuable he knows the journey will be for his son. Just because his son is going to lose everything doesn't mean the journey won't be worth anything.

Again, this is what true elders always do: release us, not control us. They resist the impulse to tell us what to do, even when we ask them to, because they know it is not good for us. Of course, when a child is young, they need simple, black-and-white rules. It is the most elemental phase of faith, where there is only law, that gives us early parameters or "containers." But the journey into maturity, into adulthood, entails trusting us to find the path for ourselves, being available for guidance, not for orders.

Unfortunately, we know that quite often the human story is that we would actually choose kings over elders, precisely because we would do anything to avoid the ambiguity and uncertainty that wise elders force us to confront within ourselves. This is what happens in the Hebrew Scriptures when the people demand, "Give us a king to judge us like all the other nations" (1 Sam. 8:5 NLT). Having a king to tell us what to do absolves us of the difficulty of learning to hear, discern, and act for ourselves, which is why it is not uncommon for people to choose even against their own freedom. Having a king is easier than having to grow up.

But God does not rule over us this way. The story of the prodigal son, a story of trying to escape down one kind of road, is instructive for how we read what happens on this other road from Jerusalem to Emmaus. The story can be read as a story of two lost disciples, and God coming to them disguised as a stranger, coming to pursue them in their lostness, as they walk away. In this way, we might see overtures of the prodigal son story—the God who looks for us. But the same section in Luke in which we get the parable of the prodigal son is where we get the parables of the lost sheep and the lost coin. The sheep that is lost is found, as is the coin. The prodigal son, too, is lost and found, but unlike the sheep and the coin, he is not sought. What's the difference? My brilliant friend Dr. Chris Green says we can't be sought because we can't actually be "lost" to the Father. We can stay close to home, like the elder son, and be lost to ourselves, or we can be far from God, like the younger son, and find ourselves.

This is why the desired end or telos of the journey can't be as simple as trying to be close to the Father's house or distant from it. It's not a story about getting nearer to or farther from the One who is never far from us but of us awakening to the presence who is always with us.

Having a king is easier than having to grow up.

What Made You Start Walking?

There is a reason why people set out on such a journey, and it is very rarely because they simply choose to. Sacred spaces bring us comfort and become deep resources of identity, community, and belonging. Not only are sacred spaces not bad, but they are also profoundly good in so many ways!

I have endless wonderful stories about encountering God in sacred spaces. I literally grew up in them—Sunday school, Sunday morning and Sunday night church, potlucks, Wednesday night Bible studies. I still have cassette tapes of the first sermons I preached to my Super Powers action figures. I brought them to church with me and kneeled on the floor to reverently reenact the wildness of Pentecost with them on padded burnt orange pews, praying each of the Justice League through to the Holy Ghost and binding the devil in the Joker and Lex Luthor. I absorbed the preaching around me into my very bones. I loved the tender fierceness of the old Pentecostal saints and the wild unrestraint of their worship, the way the rowdiness of the Spirit disrupted the power structures of the ordered world around us. I could tell you about getting lost in the wonder and dancing in the Spirit around the church for hours when I was fourteen years old, even though I came there to look at the girls.

I could tell you about bringing my Baptist girlfriend to camp meeting when I was sixteen, hoping for a tamer, calmer demonstration of the Holy Ghost, which mostly seemed to work out until the evangelist called out a man right in front of us and laid his Bible on his head, which sent him reeling on the floor. Then he asked for several "large men" to come and "get him up" so he could proceed to perform what I call the "seven-dipper" on old Brother Small. Every time he staggered back to his feet, the evangelist would hit him with the Bible again, and he'd go back to the floor. I didn't know exactly what I thought about such things, but in many ways I think I've spent my whole life trying to find the thing powerful enough to knock me flat on my back and pick me back up again.

As the road wound on for me, I found God in other spaces too. I could tell you about finding God in the shout and in the sacrament, while praying in the quiet at St. Peter's Episcopal in Charlotte or in the middle of the carnival at St. Louis Cathedral in New Orleans. I could tell you about walking onto the grounds of the Lorraine Motel in Memphis, where Dr. King was shot and where the National Civil Rights Museum is located today, and being seized with a gravity and an otherness I had not found at any of the designated holy sites in the Middle East, feeling almost thrown to the ground by them. I could tell you about how the B-3 organ at Trinity United Church of Christ in Chicago feels like the rumble of resurrection itself, making me believe it will not be the trump of Gabriel but the roar of the Hammond that will actually awaken the dead when the day comes.

I have encountered the divine in places where incense is burned and bells are rung, and also where people flail and convulse on the floor under the power of the Spirit. But it has never been a problem for people to expect God to show up in sacred spaces, whether Catholic, Orthodox, Protestant, or Pentecostal, or in any consecrated or unconsecrated spaces outside of them. Because God is in all things and fills all things, wherever you attend to the divine presence, or really even if you don't, it should be no surprise to find what you are looking for. Consecrated spaces are important precisely because we learn in reverencing one space, one meal, or one activity how we are meant to ultimately reverence all of life.

There is nothing wrong, and in fact everything right, with having a sacred space. We might even argue that everybody has to have some kind of sacred space in their life, of some sort or another. The trouble is less with having such spaces and more with the way we tend to hold them. Religious people can be notorious for confining God to the church, the temple, the mosque, the sanctuary, as if those are the only places that God is, and living as if some places are sacred and other places are not. In the worst of this, we handle only the holy person, the holy book, and the holy food with care, as if some people and some things are holy and others can be treated as profane—when in fact the very point of holding anything sacred is to learn to see the sacredness in all people and all created things. Sacred space is problematic only when religion drifts toward institutional self-preservation.

Because sacred spaces are safe spaces from which we derive a sense of belonging and identity, we are less likely to leave them than to be driven out by some sort of catastrophic event. It can be something active—as in coming into active conflict with the group or its leaders and being aggressively pushed out from the community, which is not uncommon. But it is even more common that something happens that is more subtle than being chased out of town on horseback like in an old Western, something more like an experience of heartbreaking disappointment. Something pushes you away on the inside before anything happens on the outside. Something that you hoped was true about the community you were a part of, some ideal or expectation, crash lands into disenchantment. The grief of that loss is so great that it sets you on another path. The trauma of such an event might not be as active, but it is no less devastating.

It is this kind of catastrophic disappointment that puts the two early disciples on the road to Emmaus. They thought Jesus was the One who would redeem them all, and his death seemed to prove that they were wrong all along. All of a sudden, the years of devotion and radical obedience seem utterly wasted. It is over. Their walk is not about geography but about walking away from the temple, the institution, the faith they once knew. They are walking away from God. But we've already seen this fascinating twist: the God revealed in Jesus of Nazareth is the God who will walk with you on the road away from God. They are walking away from the faith they have known and the God they have loved. And as they do, God walks alongside them, unannounced.

These disillusioned disciples did not set out on some spiritual quest for enlightenment. They didn't go looking for God. They stumbled into the truth that many people have found in a bar—in fact, people who are vulnerable with each other in a bar are far closer to a conscious awareness of the divine than those who are not vulnerable in a church—that when you get honest enough, God visits whether you invite God or not. There is something holy that happens when two humans share their deepest grief, their most jagged pain, without agenda and without pretense. There is an openness, a clarity, a freedom that comes. Spirit comes. People unlock private secrets, and where demons of addiction and shame have dominated in secrecy, light floods in and grace comes tumbling through. You don't have to pray a prayer to invoke anything. If you get honest enough, truthful enough, Love will happen in just this way, taking you by surprise.

When you get honest enough, God visits whether you invite God or not.

Many people testify to having this experience in Alcoholics Anonymous in a way they can never find in a church, precisely because AA meetings are predicated on honesty. There is a simple psychological brilliance to the movements of AA, but there is a spiritual reality to them too. When the starting point of a gathering is confession, vulnerability, and raw, unvarnished human experience, there's no wonder AA meetings are more likely to be a place to experience the reality of God than church services where the name of God is invoked a hundred times more.

And you don't have to go looking for God—you don't have to go looking for anything. If you get honest enough about the depth of your pain, the Man of Sorrows acquainted with grief will come for you, in forms you may or may not recognize. It's not really up to you to find God in any case. Trying to "find God" sounds hard. Why would you do that?

"What do you believe about God?" Questions I am not asking for $500, Alex. You can journal about that if you want to, but I'm much more interested in whether or not you have a person with whom you can process your most profound pain, your deepest trauma. Do you have a person you can talk to about when the God you knew died? When hope itself died? Do you have a person with whom you feel safe enough to name the unspeakable grief? In speaking the unspeakable, grasping for language for what we cannot name, that's when the surprise happens.

In the meantime, if you are walking away from a place that was once holy to you, I would suggest you are doing so because it was the only thing you could do, the only thing you can do. It may seem disconcerting if you don't much feel up to believing at the moment, or perhaps blasphemous if you do—but what if it was in fact God who actually sent you out on the road away from God?

That is not to say that God ordained the tragedy or is directly responsible for the pain. I do find, however, that there is no way to come to believe that God does not live in only the sacred spaces, that God is not confined to the church or the synagogue, until we become disillusioned with God there first. Counterintuitively, sometimes we have to leave the house of God in order to encounter God in the wild and to truly know there is nowhere that God is not.

All of the disciples' messianic hopes for Jesus were embodied in the sacred city of Jerusalem, and now they have to leave Jerusalem to get to Jesus. This is not a shorthand way of saying they needed to transcend their Judaism, as if Judaism was ever the problem. The earliest Christians saw themselves as a reform movement within Judaism, and with its remarkable capacity for self-critique, the Jewish tradition was always an ongoing dialectic between the priests and the prophets, who were always reminding the people of God about the ways in which God was at work on the outer edges of the tradition and the establishment. Every tradition needs both of these voices. Over against any tendency to confine God to the temple, the tradition always maintained that, in the words of Psalm 139, "If I make my bed in Sheol, you are there. If I take the wings of the morning and settle at the farthest limits of the sea, even there your hand shall lead me" (vv. 8–10).

In fact, any form of mature religion, whatever the form, like growing into adulthood, not only makes room for such a road but also requires it. The two disciples had left everything to follow Jesus. They knew about sacrifice, obedience, miracles. But they have not yet walked the path of abandonment, grief, disillusionment, and utter despair. They had the experience of faith, but they can't be trusted to lead a movement until they have shared the experience of losing it first.

When Your Hope Is Shattered

When the story gets too small, you are preoccupied with your own salvation—your way out. But then pain breaks you open into something larger. The two men are giving the stranger the business about this trauma they have experienced, what it all means to them, how there was this rabbi named Jesus who was a teacher like they had never heard before, how they had pinned all their hopes and dreams on him, how their chief priests and leaders had betrayed and crucified him. And then this sentence: "But we had hoped that he was the one to redeem Israel" (Luke 24:21).

"But we had hoped . . . " There is so much heartbreak in that phrase alone. We *had* hoped. The past perfect tense makes the sentence brutal. You can feel the sorrow and regret swimming through the words. We *had* hoped . . . but we don't dare hope anymore. We *had* hope . . . but it's gone now. There's unbearable ache in the word *had*. There is nothing more bitter than to taste hope that things will change, that things will somehow get better—only to have it ripped from you.

For them, as it is for us, there was a *particular* hope lost—not an idea or an abstract, hazy dream. They had hoped that Jesus would be the One who was going to redeem Israel. Were they wrong to have had this hope? It's a question worth exploring. In a way, I guess the Sunday school answer would be to say, "Yeah, sure, Jesus came to redeem everybody!" But I think if we look closer, what's at stake in the nature of the word *redemption* is very much in question here. In Jesus's time and in ours, there's a constant tension between those who would appropriate religious traditions in a more exclusive way and those who would do so in a more inclusive way—the question of who precisely is going to be redeemed.

The Jewish story, from the beginning, was a cosmic story big enough to embrace the whole world. What started out as a local story of one man and one family had global ambition from the very beginning. The story starts with God making a covenant with a man named Abraham, telling him he will have a great name, a great family full of sons and daughters, a great nation. But the covenant made to "Father Abraham" was always that "in you all the families of the earth shall be blessed" (Gen. 12:3). The story was always hurtling outward, wider, farther, until every family, every life would be swept up by the force of the promise God made to the one.

The scale and scope of the story, as it proceeded, were unmistakable. It was never that Abraham was God's special pet, somehow chosen over against anybody else. Rather, in the words of my friend Chris again, "the elect were chosen for the sake of the non-elect, the chosen for the sake of the non-chosen," so that ultimately the time would come when nobody would be left out.

Part of the genius of Scripture is the way it shapes our affections when we engage the sacred texts with our whole selves. When the people of God build a golden calf to worship instead of worshiping the living God, and God is getting ready to wipe them out, Moses pleads with God not to destroy them—and we are pleading too, because that is the kind of people the text is shaping us to become, people who plead, who advocate, who intercede. From a more non-Western, christological reading, we see the character of God revealed in the text through Moses himself: we recognize the one who intercedes and pleads as the God revealed in Christ. We aren't cheering for punishment but coming into alignment with the intercessor, because that is how the text works on us. Our affections are being shaped toward empathy, compassion.

Or consider when Jacob is blessed, but his brother, Esau, the original heir to the birthright, is left out. No one has ever *not* felt bad for Esau, even though it's objectively pretty dumb to give up the birthright for a bowl of stew! That's because, in the wisdom of the text, our affections are being shaped in such a way that we are *supposed* to feel bad for Esau . . . because the story was always hurtling forward toward the day when nobody would be left out of the promise God made to Abraham, the only possible outcome if truly "all the families of the earth" are blessed.

Without dismissing the "texts of terror," to use Phyllis Trible's phrase,[2] the story of Scripture, in all of its tensions, nonetheless moves forward through an ongoing dialectic between priests and prophets, clarifying the intent and the spirit of the law, which was always a tool of liberation, establishing the freedom of an oppressed people apart from their oppressors. Jesus himself then will come as the High Priest who interprets the law, in a prophetic way.

There is an extraordinary example of this dialectic in the story of the prophet Jonah. It was to no less than the great patriarch Moses himself that God gave this legendary introduction:

The LORD passed before him, and proclaimed,

> "The LORD, the LORD,
> a God merciful and gracious,
> slow to anger,
> and abounding in steadfast love and faithfulness,
> keeping steadfast love for the thousandth
>   generation,
> forgiving iniquity and transgression and sin,
> yet by no means clearing the guilty,
> but visiting the iniquity of the parents
> upon the children
> and the children's children,
> to the third and the fourth generation." (Exod.
>   34:6–7)

And the prophet Jonah, who is furious to see the promise God made to Abraham expanding right before his very eyes when he wanted to keep it constrictive, about him and his, especially when it came to a people he saw as worshiping the wrong god, throws the exact same wording from Exodus back in God's face in Jonah 4:2. He quotes the words recorded in the Torah verbatim in a windstorm of fury, except for a crucial turn. When he gets to the part where he's supposed to say "but visiting the iniquity of the parents upon the children," watch the turn: "O LORD! Is not this what I said while I was still in my own country? That is why I fled to Tarshish at the beginning; for I knew that you are a gracious God and merciful, *slow to anger, and abounding in steadfast love, and ready to relent from punishing*" (emphasis added).

This was always, always where the story was going. So much of it was always there but had been obscured under many layers from many years of reading Jewish texts in decisively non-Jewish ways. Without the rabbinic sense of dialogue, of reading the texts in dialogue, conversation, and even disputation with one another, our attempts to simply extract the "plain meaning" from a series of flat readings of Scripture, and not maintain the tension that the texts often hold, result in a contradictory mess, an incoherent jumble.

- God "is love," but hateful things would not be hateful if God did them.

- I may have to "bless my enemies," but I can appeal to the book of Judges if I want to wipe them out.

We don't have the resources to see the story the stories are telling us. We still want God to punish our enemies, not seeing that the stories of judgment in Scripture actually show us that the kind of punishments we would want wouldn't actually change anything. To return to my friend Chris again, he puts it provocatively: "The texts of judgment are there to show us that judgment doesn't work, even if God does it." The pattern that we see repeatedly in the Hebrew Bible is that whenever the God character in the text acts in vengeance—for example, when the sons of Korah are swallowed up by the earth (Num. 16:32)—not only do the people keep on doing whatever wicked things they did before, but they also generally get even worse. If punishment doesn't work for God, why would we think it would work for us?

The narrow way of love is truly the narrow way, so when the people of God face resistance or something far more damning, there is always a temptation to drift from the wide-screen, sweeping hope for people into a smaller, more exclusive hope for me and mine. Some of Jesus's own disciples had not yet gotten beyond the imagination of an uprising against a violent Roman occupation that would vindicate Israel over against her oppressors. If that is what it means for Jesus to come and "redeem" Israel, then Jesus never redeems Israel.

Jesus never redeems Israel in the form the disciples were looking for, and he still hasn't!

When the disciples say, "We had hoped that he was the one to redeem Israel" (Luke 24:21), they are only half right. The harrowing, staggering truth was that Jesus was coming to redeem *everybody*. Jesus was coming to redeem both the oppressed and the oppressors. The scale and scope of what he had come to do were beyond their reckoning. Redemption would come not in the form of a sword to defeat their enemies but in the shape of a cross. In other words, not in the form of triumph over the so-called enemies of God but in the shape of nonviolent, self-giving love.

The trouble with the hope they had before the road away from God was that it was simply yet too small. It was too small, too narrow, too self-interested. The painful truth was there was going to be no path to that wider, broader, bigger hope without having their smaller, more constricting hope utterly shattered. In order for them to be broken open to a broader, more expansive view of God and the world, they were going to have to walk the path of godforsakenness first. Only this path of disorientation, disillusionment, and questioning could open them up to the surprise of everything, where they could finally be restored to what had been the arc and trajectory of true faith all along: a hope big enough for all the families of the earth.

Everybody's hope is too small—before they suffer. It is only suffering that breaks us open and allows us to see our too-small hope for "me/mine/us" and the possibility of a hope that could be big enough for "them."

One Person's Apostasy Is Another Person's Revival

This is always the human tendency in religion: over time, what was supposed to be a sweeping, universal story, an anthem big enough for all of creation, gets turned into a ditty only a select few can sing. Jesus is the One who comes along to remind the two disciples of what God has actually been up to in the story all along. Jesus *was* the One to redeem Israel—but that was a way of saying, "We thought he was coming for 'us.'" The scandalous truth was that he had come every bit as much for "them." And that's still the way the story works: Jesus comes for "us" and also for "them," and not only that, but he comes to erase the artifice of separateness that once distinguished "us" and "them." Using language more radical than anyone in his world was prepared for, the apostle Paul says that in Christ, "there is no longer Jew or Greek, there is no longer slave or free, there is no longer male and female; for all of you are one in Christ Jesus" (Gal. 3:28).

It's ironic that Jesus shows the disciples how they are only half right, and so many people now are only half right about Jesus. They may get some things about the message of Jesus and the story of Jesus as it has been handed down through the witness of the church technically right. But as it was in Jesus's time, what was intended to be faith with cosmic, universal scope has become small and petty, precisely because we, too, have become a people preoccupied with our own salvation. And when people become preoccupied with their own salvation, the only way to rid themselves of such an overriding concern is often to "lose it"—to walk that disenchanted, disillusioned road from Jerusalem to Emmaus.

The disciples, though, are on this road because they have already been driven onto the road of grief and despair, where new life might yet be possible. They have already lost everything, and have nothing left to lose. Not everyone is on this path. For people who are still within the safety of the sacred city, those walking this road don't look like pilgrims but apostates. The story may be narrated merely as children rejecting their faith; friends may see their peers and colleagues as merely rejecting their tradition.

Disillusionment and disenchantment push us out of comfort and to the margins, where God always is. This is a road that often must be walked so that the Spirit can be experienced outside of the tame and false politeness of the gatekeepers, who would claim to tell us where, when, and on whom God is able to move. Breaking away from them is not breaking away from God but can be a breaking away *into* God.

This is not my tome on North American Christianity, but even people with a peripheral understanding of the Jesus story can recognize that white evangelicalism, in particular, has gone far from the way of Christ. In such a time, one person's idea of walking away is my idea of a revival. In the ways in which people walk away from a Christianity that has become petty, small, constricting, and compromised, I see a walk toward the resurrected One. And ironically, it seems to me that it is the God they worshiped in the church in the sacred city who has made them too restless to stay with the people who insist that God can be found only there.

I am at this point far more concerned about those who never push against the boundaries of the institution than those who follow the summons to explore the world outside of it, because I know that the Jesus who was crucified "outside the city gate" (Heb. 13:12) roams these streets. The truth is that a faith system that loses touch with God's heart for "all the families of the earth" and actively stirs people to be over against their neighbors rather than to join the Son of love in sacrifice for them is not a faith that needs to be tweaked but a faith that needs to die.

> **Disillusionment and disenchantment push us out of comfort and to the margins, where God always is.**

I do not mean this as a mere positive spin but as a matter of absolute conviction: I see the deep disillusionment so many people have right now with the church and religion as a sign not of falling away but of deeper fidelity to God. They rightly recognize that a story too small to embrace all of creation is simply not big enough, so they set off on the road in search of one. I am convinced that the author of such a story—expansive, playful, and full of mischief—is all too eager to be found.

4

Your Pain Is Real

IN CASE ANY OF THIS talk of going and leaving to walk the road feels glib, let's take a moment to really sit with the reality of any of these kinds of transitions: not only are they often painful, but they can also be excruciating. In fact, our sense of belonging is so deeply tied to our communities and the communities that shaped us that any sort of fracturing from them may well seem unsurvivable. It feels like leaving may actually kill us, and there is a kind of truth to that—the places that have most shaped our deepest sense of identity and belonging become such a part of our emotional, spiritual, and psychological well-being that being displaced from them can be as disorienting, severe, and outright heartbreaking as death. There is a very real way in which a part of us dies.

Many of the people I am closest to in the world have endured cataclysmic rejection from their families of origin precisely because they are walking the road. Not merely judgment, not just criticism, but a violent, brutal severing that likely cannot be undone in this life. The effects of this pain in the moment are not just sad but shattering. There is really no way to overstate just how painful that loss of belonging or "home" can be.

Society gives us few resources to help us weather this kind of grief, and few spaces in which it is safe to grieve. Inevitably, we want someone to tell us that there is a path to new life, to some kind of resurrection, that does not go this way of grief and death. This is where the Jesus story in general and the Emmaus story in particular notably do not offer any shortcuts. God takes no delight in our suffering, and the way of Jesus does not regard suffering for its own sake as having some intrinsic virtue. But the One who bore the cross did not simply bear it for us as a representative. Instead, he comes to show us that the way of death and resurrection is the only way for us as well. Thus, he tells us, "Take up [your] cross daily and follow me" (Luke 9:23).

It is fascinating that this is often translated as a fairly random call to some radical act of self-denial or into a life of ascetic practices rather than its more obvious meaning: what makes the cross "the cross" is not the extreme physical suffering or the pain of self-denial, generally, but the throbbing, acute rejection at the hands of a community we once called our own. This is the central genius of René Girard's illuminating work on Job, calling him "the victim of his people."[1] It is the social consequence of feeling despised, rejected, and cut off by his community that makes Job's pain unbearable. In this regard, it makes plenty of sense why most of us would rather contort ourselves in superfluous acts of self-denial any day than bear the pain of feeling disapproved of by our community.

Unfortunately, there is no path to resurrection and new life that does not go the way of this pain, at least on some level. People who never experience this pain of rejection, who avoid being alienated from the herd at all costs, are rarely able to come into maturity emotionally or spiritually. It is certainly more convenient to avoid such pain altogether, but the cost is often that the life we live does not fully feel like our own. The Emmaus narrative reveals how the same story that proclaims the good news of the resurrection also proclaims, with equal voice, this: *your pain is real, and it cannot be diminished.*

What the Prophets Have Spoken

Finally, the stranger speaks. But what erupts is not empathy. Neither is it frustration but mirth, playfulness: "So thick-headed! So slow-hearted! Why can't you simply believe all that the prophets said? Don't you see that these things had to happen, that the Messiah had to suffer and only then enter into his glory?" (Luke 24:25–26 MSG). He takes the men off guard. They had shared a pain so raw and personal, it would be understandable if they responded to him with something like rage. But the stranger is so winsome. He displays such wit, such intelligence, such a deep sense of knowing, as if he is not dismissing their pain but is somehow big enough to carry it, hold it, yet play with it.

From there the man launches into a lecture on the Torah unlike anything they have ever heard before. Only it isn't really a lecture; it is a tour de force, it is jazz music, it is a living, fiery, fearsome thing. The stranger talks about the law of Moses as if he knew Moses. He takes it from the top, from Moses on the mountain, down through all the prophets, who spoke the wild truth of God from the outer edges of things.

And while he talks, everything is being illuminated— the Scriptures, their lives, the very path beneath their feet as they walk. And not only are things lighting up, but they are also being connected, forming a tapestry of light. Everything is connected, everything is being connected, they are being connected. It is as if he is putting the pieces of the story together, the pieces of their own stories are coming together, they themselves are coming together.

These things had to happen, the stranger says. All of that pain, all of that heartbreak, all of that sorrow, the very things that have ripped them apart—these things had to happen. But the point is not that the stranger is revealing a God who is playing chess with their lives and the lives of everyone they love. The point is not that there is a cosmic script. The stranger is illuminating what the prophets said.

And what did the prophets say? The Hebrew prophets said a lot of things. They warned the people of God over and over about the consequences of trusting in their own resources, of militarism and nationalistic power, of economic wealth. They warned what would happen if they mistreated the alien, the refugee, the widow, if they ignored the voices on the outer edges of things. They reminded the people that their God was not indifferent to injustice and to the cries of the oppressed. Prophets, of their time and ours, hold a mirror up to us,

The way of death is the way to life. The way of pain is bound up in the way of joy.

show us ourselves and the world as both truly are, show us the inevitability of what is to come if we do not change our ways.

And then, there is also that terrible truth that the path to redemption has always gone the way of suffering. All prophets intuitively know this, and we have always hated them for it. They are unlike the false prophets, who speak "'Peace, peace,' when there is no peace" (Jer. 6:14). We are desperate for someone to tell us if there's a way out and if there's a way forward that does not go the way of suffering. But there has always been a kind of inevitability to suffering, not because God sadistically insists on it but because death and resurrection are embedded in everything in the cosmos. The way of death is the way to life. The way of pain is bound up in the way of joy.

Don't you see it always had to be this way? That there was always going to be no going around, only straight through? When Jesus gets to that bit in the prophet Isaiah about being "despised and rejected of men" (Isa. 53:3 KJV), why does it slice right through them? And when he quotes from that same passage about "a man of sorrows and acquainted with grief," there is something jagged but unbearably tender about the way he says those words. He seems more than casually acquainted with grief himself—he carries himself like he's known more than his share of sorrows. "But he was wounded for our transgressions, crushed for our iniquities . . . " (v. 5). However lyrical his voice sounds in the desert, the weight of those words on his lips is so heavy that the two men can't help but shift their eyes to the ground as he says them.

He is blazing through the Torah, through texts, through tradition, through their very souls. Through Moses, through Ezekiel, through David, through major prophets and minor prophets, major chords and minor chords. It is law and it is history. It is as sultry as the Song of Songs and as bluesy as the Psalms and as apocalyptic as the book of Daniel and as heartbreaking as the book of Lamentations. But what is most laid bare is the book of their own lives. What is most laid bare is their own ineffable longing. And it is all connecting—the words from the scrolls and the words from the stranger and the words from the conversation chock-full of heartbreak that they had been having just moments before. All of it is lighting up. And how could they have imagined, when everything inside of them had died, that from this one conversation with this strange man with the radioactive dark eyes that all of a sudden they could feel so alive again?

The Day After

One of the things I love most about this story is that it inhabits that ambiguous space between death and resurrection. With startling precision, it speaks to the pain we all feel in these liminal spaces, between what we've loved and what we've lost. We have little common language for lament in the public square when it comes to the worst days of our lives, perhaps even less for these shadowy in-between spaces. Sometimes the thing you thought you couldn't survive is not the hardest thing to survive. The truth is we can survive more than we think we can, more than we thought we should, perhaps more than we'd even want to. People survive the unsurvivable every day. The real monster is false hope. When you thought you saw shore, but it was only an illusion. When you thought you found a miracle, but it was only a mirage. When you thought you found an oasis, but there was only more sand. When you thought you hit the bottom, but you fell deeper still. When you thought you found your people, but they didn't turn out to be your people. When you thought you found a new home, but it was just another pit stop on an unending journey. When you thought you heard God, but it was only an echo of your own voice.

It's not the suffering that threatens to destroy you. It's the heartbreak that comes when you think you've made it out but haven't.

And even then, it is not the day of this dark discovery that takes you out with the tide.

It's the day after.

Holy Saturday

The in-between space can seem to stretch into the infinite. You think you must be at the end of the record, that there surely cannot be more—but it seems to just keep going, and going, and going. How many times have I been certain that I had grieved a thing, let go of a thing, released a thing, was ready to let go into that newness and make room for resurrection—only to find that there were just more miles of the same?

If this is a road trip through Nebraska or the Dakotas or that lonely highway in Nevada, and it is miles and miles of relative geographic sameness, I am happy to crank up Bruce Springsteen and romanticize it. I am inclined to try anything within my power to fast-forward my way past the in-between at all costs. I want to move through, move on, get to the next thing. I want to will my way out, write my way out, whatever I have to do. It's really hard to know where you are in a process when you have so many reasons for wanting to convince yourself you are done with the process altogether.

But there's a reason why we aren't supposed to skip straight to Easter. There is a rhythm to the liturgical calendar, a rhythm to Holy Week, like there's a rhythm to the seasons. I need the space of Good Friday to make room for all that is dead and dying. But in recent years, especially, I have come to love often neglected Holy Saturday because it gives language for that in-between space where I live so much of my life but I often don't know how to name. It reminds me there is room for this kind of space in the resurrection story, and in the ongoing story of my life—that it is part of the consecrated story. It reminds me that in-between space is sanctified space.

The disciples have lived through the worst of it—but they have not yet entered into the full awareness that resurrection is about to summon them into. For now, they are still in that hazy in-between space, where it feels like nothing is happening yet but anything could. The encounter with the stranger itself is hard to quantify. They do not know the identity of their interlocutor. The ancestor Jacob wrestled all night in the shadows with . . . an angel . . . with God? The in-between is a dark, ambiguous place.

Perhaps you, like these two disciples, sense that the road is leading somewhere, to a moment of awareness, to a moment of seeing. Maybe even with all the pain, sorrow, and trauma of the road thus far, you have not yet given up hope for your own kind of revelation. But you don't know until you know, so for now, you must take comfort in the grace of in-between spaces.

I wrote the following meditation for Holy Saturday, but the beauty of the church's liturgical calendar is that you get to apply this grace to any day as needed. Make this Saturday a Holy Saturday if need be. Death and resurrection are happening literally all the time, and all the time there is a gentle whisper running through us and beneath us that summons us to a place where all things are made new.

> There is grace this Holy Saturday for all kinds of in-between spaces.
> There is grace this Holy Saturday for not being who you were but not yet being who you are to become.
> There is grace this Holy Saturday for those in the liminal, shadowy place between crucifixion and resurrection.
> There is grace this Holy Saturday for those in between sleeping and waking, grieving and dancing, heartbreak and hope.
> There is grace this Holy Saturday for not knowing, for holding tension, for being unsure, for making a bed in the belly of a whale.
> There is grace this Holy Saturday to rest, be still, and know or not know.
> Because resurrection doesn't depend on you or need your permission.[2]

From Earthquake to Jailbreak

One of the things I cherish most about the Jesus story, and the Jesus tradition, is that it forces us to reckon with the truth of death in a time when we work so hard and so often to live in complete denial of it. But what the Jesus story does not do, and in fact does not allow us to do, is glamorize suffering for its own sake. In fact, if we are able to romanticize suffering, it is a sure sign we know next to nothing about it. In the Jesus story, death is not a friend to be cooperated with but an ultimate enemy to be overthrown. Death is not the aim or the destination but rather the necessary passage into newness. Jesus himself "for the sake of the joy that was set before him endured the cross, disregarding its shame" (Heb. 12:2).

While it may be helpful to have a full moratorium on men using birth metaphors, the pain of childbirth is the absolute center of the universal pattern: no new life comes into the world without tremendous pain. But the excruciating pain is still chosen, not as an end unto itself but for the unimaginable joy of the new life on the other side of it. I walk real soft if I talk about birthing babies, because I know absolutely nothing about it experientially. But I do know that, as it is in birth, the means by which we break out of small spaces into the wildness of life on the other side is also marked by a kind of violence, and in the moment people are often uncertain if they will survive it.

The Bible is full of these stories of survival, including a strange story not often told from the book of Acts about an earthquake.

The apostle Paul and his companion, Silas, are preaching the good news about Jesus of Nazareth when a demon-possessed girl starts to follow them around. The spirit that controls her also gives her supernatural insight into the future, so her gift has created a minor cottage industry in her little town that brings good business to the people who exploit her. As she follows after them, she cries out with a loud voice, "These men are servants of the Most High God!" (Acts 16:17 NIV). Day in and day out, she continues to follow them, yelling these words to the crowds. Finally, the apostle Paul whips around, irritated, and simply casts the demon out of the girl.

This whole subplot is fascinating to me, precisely because the girl does not proclaim anything that is not technically true. Paul and Silas are in fact servants of the Most High God, worth giving attention to. Evidently, though, it is possible for the wrong spirit to say the right thing—which is why there are an awful lot of loud voices crying out these days, stacking Bible verses underneath everything they say, even citing chapter and verse, that we should clearly identify as demonic, incendiary, destructive, and distracting. This is why 1 John 4:1 tells us to "test the spirits": the "truth" of God is not located entirely in "the facts" but in the tender and gentle heart of Christ. Thus, tone matters, spirit matters, disposition matters, intention matters—not just the technical veracity of the words.

Paul casts the demon out of the girl, which silences the spirit's manic ranting and sets her free from its oppression but also jeopardizes the livelihood of the townsfolk who were profiteering by exploiting her bondage. There is another sermon for another time, perhaps, but worth mentioning: people are always fine if you talk about Jesus so long as you don't challenge their money or their wars, as these are the two places from which we as a people derive our meaning. And thus, no matter how secular or even pluralistic we might become, these are the two idols we still hold sacred.

This little episode enrages the crowd, who turn Paul and Silas over to the Roman police. They are badly beaten and then thrown into a tiny Macedonian jail cell. Paul is the apostle to the gentiles, the one designated to bring the good news of the Jewish Messiah to all outside the household of Israel. But now he and Silas are locked inside a small space. In a very real sense, the gospel itself is locked inside that small space.

Around midnight, this pair of bedraggled disciples begin singing their praises to God. And as they do, an earthquake comes. Specifically, the text says, "The foundations of the prison were shaken" (Acts 16:26). As I was rereading this story, I was conscious of the fact that in our own time, the very foundations are shaking—political systems, ecclesiastical systems, fundamental belief systems. Everything that seemed unshakable is shaking.

For Paul and Silas, I have to imagine that when the shaking began, their first thought was not, *Oh, good.*

Our deliverer has come. I have to think that after a full day of being flogged and beaten and thrown into stocks in a tiny cell, the sight of the walls themselves seeming to give way did not seem like an ideal ending to a very bad day. Like the people of God in Haggai, these disciples had been "shaken" enough.

As it is with any earthquake, the shaking is indiscriminate; it is violent. Things that we think should and should not be shaken are both shaken, and there's nothing we can do to stop it. The overriding sensation is of powerlessness, our complete lack of control. Religion makes no difference at all as to whether or not the shaking comes—the shaking comes to us all, no matter what we believe about it theologically or philosophically.

> **The shaking comes to us all, no matter what we believe about it theologically or philosophically.**

And yet, the earthquake that seems like it will kill them is the very thing that God uses to set them free. The earthquake actually releases Paul and Silas from their chains! What is experienced as an earthquake for everybody else is actually a jailbreak for Paul and Silas. It is again an occasion when everyone experiences the same shaking, but God's people perceive some particular purpose in the shaking.

There are so many foundations that are crumbling these days, so much so quickly, that I could not begin to assert with any authority that I know what in these violent winds is the Spirit's work. But in all that is falling down, this conviction is clear to me: many people with buried treasure have been locked inside some very small spaces, and whatever forces are shaking them up are shaking them loose. What would seem to be an agent of destruction the Spirit may use as an instrument to usher them into terrible freedom.

So many children of the church, like the men in this story, have been stuck inside small, constricting, confining spaces. And the pain of that is real; the pain of that is something Jesus knows intimately. The shaking that happens and threatens to take them out—it is a violent, disruptive shaking that threatens the very foundations of reality. It is not in the character of God to send the disaster, but it is in God's very job description to engineer beauty out of the disastrous. The very shaking that seems like it will kill you may be the very thing the Spirit leverages to set you free.

5

It's Good to Be a Fan

OFTEN, IT'S THE TOXIC VOICES from toxic spaces that send us walking to begin with. But to turn this question on its head, what voices speak in a way that brings you life right now? In what spaces do you find the truth your soul longs to hear? Are they different voices or different spaces than the ones that mattered to you before? Is there a summons of the Spirit in your yearning that wants to break you open to a broader way of seeing God and of seeing your neighbor?

Not all guides are wise guides, and even the ones who are wise are not equally wise or equally helpful for every part of the journey. You may be at a place where some of the voices that spoke into your life before are not serving you for where you are on the journey now. You get to change the channel. That doesn't mean you have to dismiss anything good or valuable you ever gleaned from them before.[1] You get to take the things with you that you need to take with you and not take the things with you that you don't.

But there are times in the transition when you actually do need to unsubscribe, for the moment—to stop listening. And there are moments when you know you have a hunger for voices that are established, mature voices in the spiritual life. If you need some kind of permission slip telling you it's okay to look elsewhere to find the wise guides that you need for the person you know you can and must become, then consider this your permission slip.

You get to decide whether it's time to walk away from some voices altogether or to say, as the disciples do to the unknown stranger on the Emmaus road, "Stay with us."

Stay with Us

You never know who you might encounter on the road. We do know that God often comes to us in the guise of a stranger and that being open to the surprise gift of an unexpected human presence is one of the primary ways we open ourselves more fully to the divine presence that is always with us.

The Emmaus story demonstrates the incredulity of this stranger narrative like nothing else. So the disciples finally get to the edge of the village where they are headed, and the stranger acts "as if" he is going on. Those two little words are two of my favorites within the text, because if you still haven't gotten an idea yet of the playfulness of Jesus, of the twinkle in his eye, of his mischief—behold the Lamb of God, who pranks his disciples. I'm convinced that's mostly what resurrection looks like anyway: God punking us. I don't mean this in a mean-spirited way, of course, but in the way of ultimate, audacious surprise. God comes to us in a form we couldn't have expected, at a time we couldn't have expected, in a way that is likely to be as equally hilarious as it is beautiful.[2]

"As if." In other words, the stranger has no intention of going farther. He is absolutely winding them up. He's enjoying himself. He's having a good time. "Well, I guess I really should be going," he says. Ah, but here is a truly beautiful part of the text. The two men don't yet have any idea who they're talking to. They are still not aware of the miracle that's unfolding before them. They don't have the revelation yet, full recognition yet. All they know is that in the course of their conversation, something has come alive in them again and they don't want it to end.

I'm convinced that's mostly what resurrection looks like: God punking us.

Have you had one of those magical moments when you didn't know exactly what it was or what to call it but something inside you said yes to whatever it was? You didn't have to know what to name it; you didn't have to put language around it. It was deeper than words. You just knew you wanted more of whatever it was. I think about when my grandmother would visit the house when I was a little boy, and when I sensed it was time for her to leave, I would beg her to stay . . . just ten more minutes.

That's the two disciples here. *Won't you just stay here for a little while longer?* They aren't looking for a commitment; they don't know who they're talking to or what to ask for . . . *just please, please don't go—not yet.*

Since the One who walks with you has an essence that is not just loving but *is* Love, you hardly have to write up a formal invitation.[3] But there is something sweet about that moment of invitation, that first tiny movement toward surrender to Love who calls you by your true name—however unadorned that moment may be. It is the moment when there may not yet be intellectual clarity, but there is a deep recognition within that something is happening in your life that you aren't ready to be over. Would you stay with me . . . *for just a little while longer?*

I don't know if you are one for prayer books or prayers in general, but if you feel like hurtling a prayer out there, you could join with me in reciting this reimagined prayer of the men who walked the road away from God but found themselves open to the surprise of a stranger.

> I do not know what this is.
> I do not know who you are
> or what you are,
> but there is something about this.

There is something about now
that knows that this is GOOD.
There is something about this.
There is something about now
that makes my soul say . . .
YES,
however tentatively.
YES,
to whatever this is,
to whatever you are,
to whatever is happening.
Would you stay here,
for just a little while longer?

Their intuition is not from head knowledge; it's not intellectual certainty. It's not clarity about the road ahead. It's a guttural, stomach-and-bone kind of recognition that whatever is in front of them now is good, a knowing that they have to welcome the present moment with their whole selves.

More often than not, it is a knowing—as it was for these two disciples—that the road is a lonely one, and we do well to travel it in good company when we can. We do well to welcome the person in front of us, those walking the same direction, with our whole selves. That's the movement in all these sacred stories—the surprise that comes in welcoming a stranger as a friend, or finding yourself surprised by such a welcome.

We may find that in welcoming the stranger, we are welcoming God. Or we may find God by allowing ourselves to be in the vulnerable posture of being received as the stranger ourselves. Saul of Tarsus, a terrorist to early followers of Jesus, was blinded by a light on the road to Damascus. God sent a man named Ananias, one of the very people Saul had been actively persecuting, to the house where he was staying. But instead of being greeted with suspicion, Saul the terrorist is greeted as "*Brother* Saul" (Acts 22:13). It is only when his enemy greets him as a friend and says "regain your sight" that Saul's eyes are opened like those of a newborn baby, and he can finally begin to rightly discern the world around him.

It is of course a terrifying thing to be received in this way, to take the risk of loving and being loved by one we once thought of as our enemy. But this is how relationship with God always works, and it directly correlates to relationships with others—the unfolding that happens within us when we allow ourselves to unfold with others.

So much hinges on whether or not we are able to come to recognize the face of Christ in the face of another human. And when we do—especially on the road away from God—it can feel like a homecoming. The disciples had no idea who they were talking to at first, but they sensed the comfort of kinship. And isn't this what we're all looking for, especially after all we've lost?

People We Believe In

I understand that God is the One in whom we put our faith in an *ultimate* sense, but in a very real way, we will believe in God only to the extent that we can believe in others. I read something from Rowan Williams fifteen years ago that I have actually thought about every week since:

> Belief in God starts from a sense that we "believe in," we trust some kinds of people. We have confidence in the way they live; the way they live is the way I want to live, perhaps can imagine myself living in my better or more mature moments. The world they inhabit is one we'd like to live in. Faith has a lot to do with the simple fact that there are trustworthy lives to be seen, that we can see in some believing people a world we'd like to live in.[4]

All this talk of welcoming and being welcomed by the stranger isn't just metaphor. This is usually how it works: we are able to grow in our awareness spiritually only to the extent that we are willing to open ourselves up to loving and being loved by other people. This is why the language of "the body of Christ" is so crucial, and certainly not just relegated to some kind of institution. The way we relate to other corporeal bodies, the way we connect to each other, is a significant part of how we connect to God.

We are able to grow in our awareness spiritually only to the extent that we are willing to open ourselves up to loving and being loved by other people.

It is certainly not the only way. There are many forms of prayer, and really any way of being in the world with God is prayer. I have had plenty of those moments in nature when I felt connected to whatever current holds it all together, holds all created things—holds me together too. I have had experiences that have been strange and spooky that made me want to believe in some kind of deeper mystery, and occasionally made me terrified of it.

But there is still rarely anything that ever happens to me that is as truly miraculous as the strangers I meet on the road and the ways in which we find each other, the ways we find shelter in each other and in each other's stories. Nothing is as mysterious as these other bodies—somebody, anybody, everybody—who end up walking alongside us, how they got to us and how we got to them.

I used to have to listen to people who came through my circles doing apologetics—attempting to do some sort of intellectual defense of Christianity—an exercise that was mind-numbingly awful even at the time. I once sat through a painful series of seminars given by a man who taught us "ten ways to prove the Bible is true without using Scripture." I couldn't imagine even then why on earth anyone would be interested in either of those things—proving the Bible is true and needing to carefully avoid using an actual sacred text to do so. I can summarize basically all of his points for you: "The disciples were martyred for their faith and didn't renounce Jesus, meaning the resurrection of Christ is an absolute, scientific fact. BOOM-SHAKALAKA."

This is followed by a handy script you can use on your unbelieving neighbors. You ask, "Hey, neighbor, do you believe in propositional truth?" And because your neighbor is likely a godless heathen, they will likely respond with, "Why no, as a matter of fact, I do not believe in absolute truth. I believe all truth is relative." At which point you say, "Haha! Saying you don't believe in absolute truth *is* an absolute statement, which means your logic is flawed. Now renounce your sins and make Jesus your personal Lord and Savior. BOOM-SHAKALAKA." And the deal is signed. (Thanks, everyone, for attending my apologetics seminar!)

I simply do not believe that is how faith works. Contra a popular apologetics book from way back when, I have yet to see any evidence that "demands" any sort of verdict, only an invitation to a loving response. I'm also ever mindful of Marilynne Robinson's searing line from *Gilead*: "Nothing true about God can be said from a posture of defense."[5] I also think of the words of my mentor at Duke, Stanley Hauerwas, spoken in his imitable Texas twang: "If you need a system to prop up your belief in Jesus of Nazareth, then worship your system, because you don't worship Jesus of Nazareth."

If pressed for my own "reason" for believing in Jesus (if I am supposed to give one beyond being endlessly compelled by the tender fierceness I have found in the figure of Jesus, and a handful of people who have mediated the story of Jesus to me in a profound way), here it is: God revealed through nonviolent, sacrificial, self-giving love is the best ground floor for reality I can find in a literary, poetic, and philosophical way. But mostly, it has been much more simple than that: I believe in God the way that I do because there are people, "some kinds of people," I have believed in, have put trust in.

As with those disciples on the road, that hasn't meant I have always understood the presence, weight, gravitas, groundedness, or tenderness I have witnessed in some of the strangers I've encountered. Nor does it mean that I have romanticized or sentimentalized the people in whom I have seen these things or that I needed them to be rid of basic human complexity. Yet I still find it is mostly through the portal of human lives that I see glimpses of "a world I would like to live in."

By now, you probably have a clear sense of whose world you *don't* want to live in, and this is valuable information! It's good to know what needs renouncing, what is over the line for you, what sent you walking to begin with. It's good to know these are not your people. But to follow this essential knowledge with more questions: If you know where you don't want to be, where *do* you want to live? Who *are* your people? What vision of reality compels you? What kindred spirits can you find who are hoping for this world with you? In other words, as you look to your left and to your right, who is walking with you on the road, perhaps in the same direction? And can you find it in yourself to reach out to them?

It's Good to Be a Fan

They say, "Don't meet your heroes" (because apparently "they" are crusty ol' cynics), but okay, I get it: anybody put on a pedestal is destined to be knocked off, and it's not good to put others on them or to be put on one . . . a raw deal for everybody involved. But while conceding pedestal-building is universally bad business, I actually do want to put in a good word for being a fan, in general. I think the scales generally still tilt toward it being a good idea to be a supporter, an enthusiast, loving intensely, even taking into account the times we get burned. I have met an awful lot of people on this road who have mediated something of Christ to me, who have surprised me, and I have a long list of people and stuff I unashamedly go all fanboy over.

I am mostly a fan of the people I live my life with, but for the moment, let's keep it broad, just because being a pop culture fan is fun. I perk up whenever a person starts telling a story about encountering for the first time in real life someone (whether famous or not) who has had a significant influence on them, someone who has had a hold over their imagination. People love celebrity encounters in part because they serve as a kind of Rorschach test: we project so much of our own hopes and dreams onto such persons that if we ever collide with them in real life, what we see, hear, and feel surely says as much about us as it does about them. There is a kind of revealing that happens in those moments.

When it comes to meeting my *heroes,* I am genuinely the most uncool, excruciatingly embarrassing person imaginable. Regrettably, I could give you a handful of examples, but I'll tell just two. Once, when I was at the White House reception for the opening of the Museum of African American History and Culture, I looked over my shoulder and saw *the* Samuel L. Jackson and just about stopped breathing. After twenty minutes or so of talking myself up, I finally approached this icon in his elegant, chocolate-brown suit, and this is what came out: "Umm . . . Mr. Jackson? My name is Jonathan Martin, and I'm such a big fan of yours. Like a *huge fan* of yours. I mean, I know everybody is a fan, but not like me—I'm a . . . I'm a megafan." And there was this moment, before he generously agreed to take a photo with this giggling giant white man, when he raised his eyebrows in that bemused smirky way that only Samuel L. Jackson can, and he simply repeated back to me, "Ohhhhhh . . . a *mega*fan?" And for a split second, I regretted my entire existence. But, uncool or not, there is a truthfulness to geeking out about something, from train sets to action figures to meeting a professional wrestler you loved in 1972.

Then there was the time my dream of meeting Bono, me being the over-the-top U2 fan that I am, actually came true.

After years of failed schemes (I am too clumsy and obtrusive for stalking), I finally got my chance. I had been doing some volunteer work on the faith side for

the ONE Campaign, Bono's nonprofit, and my friend
from the ONE Campaign invited me to a dinner with
some other faith-leader types before a U2 show in 2017.
There were no guarantees I would get to meet him,
but my hopes were high.

Steven, one of my best friends, was speaking at a
church a couple of hours away that weekend, so I invited him to come with me. At least this time I wasn't
shuffling my feet in the corner and muttering to myself like a serial killer. I had somebody to talk to, but
I also had more time to get in my head on this one,
especially thinking I would have a couple of moments
to tell the artist who had most influenced me something of what his work had meant. I was freaking out
about this to Steven. "I definitely know I am not going
to be cool. Should I find a way to at least attempt to
be cool?" Steven said something I thought was wise.
Because we both have done this work of writing and
speaking, he said, "We both know on a smaller level
what it means when somebody says something genuine
about how something we have said has impacted them.
Why would you not want that to be felt, even if it was
awkward? I say just be who you are!"

Bono's assistant walked us to the makeshift green-
room backstage in the stadium, and I was already losing composure. And as Steven and I were talking and
laughing, so help me, I could *feel* him walk in . . . five
feet six inches of rock 'n' roll genius, and even with
my back turned, I froze the way a rabbit does when you
come upon one in your yard.

When the moment came, playing it cool was not an option, because one of the guys pointed out to Bono the tattoo of the black suitcase with a red heart in it on my inside forearm, an icon from U2's *All That You Can't Leave Behind* album. That tattoo marked a sacred experience: after not riding a bicycle in over twenty-five years, one day I found myself back on a bike riding in circles the way I did when I was eight years old. It was like the muscle memory of it made me remember who I was then . . . unencumbered by any other identity or expectation, utterly free, when imagination, prayer, and wonder were my mother tongue.

And while having this moment on my bike, with U2 on my headphones, Bono was singing the words of the stranger over me again, singing about losing your life to find it: "Sky falls, you feel like it's a beautiful day." I felt the truth of the words in a way that was more true than anything had ever been before. For the first time in my life, down in my belly, I knew that whatever death was, it truly wasn't the end, that some part of me was going to go on forever. The Edge's guitar was chiming, and Bono's vocals were soaring into my consciousness. That night on my bike I wept for hours at the beauty of God and of innocence restored.

Now *that* little Irish man was standing in front of me. I laughed, in a mixture of self-deprecation and authentic humiliation, and said, "Hey, I am aware that back here it is very uncool to have a band-related tattoo, but your music has carried me through so much. I am unabashedly that fan right now." And in a way that was perfect both because he accepted rather than deflected my affectionate geekiness and because he lowered the temperature, the man who sings the melodies I have hung my life on gently touched my arm and said in a lyrical Bono way, "You don't need to ever apologize for being a fan. I am still a fan of people whose art and music inspire me. That's the posture you want to live all of your life from. As a fan. It's *good* to be a fan." I've never stopped thinking about that line.

> "You don't need to ever apologize for being a fan. . . . That's the posture you want to live all of your life from. As a fan. It's good to be a fan." —Bono

We also had a very short conversation about preachers. "I feel like singers and preachers have a lot in common," he said. "We are both always looking for that top-line melody in the room." And he talked about how people of faith across left and right should stand up to the injustice and open madness of Trumpism. Whenever anybody else would say something and I figured out some small way to interject, I would kind of blurt it out like a character in an *SNL* sketch. So when one of the guys said, "Jonathan here reckons that Steven is one of the best preachers in America," I said in all caps, "OH, HE IS. HE IS!!!" And when Bono's assistant, who had been politely trying to pull him away for five minutes, finally said, "Bono, we really have to go," I one last time, in a way that evidently sounded both hypersincere and enthusiastic but also had the inflection of a bad Elvis impersonation, turned back around and blurted out, "Thank you, Bono. THANKYOUsooomuch." Ten minutes later, Larry Mullen Jr. was laying down the drum intro to "Sunday Bloody Sunday," and Bono walked out onstage . . . and I was a little child swept up in the ocean.

But what lingers most still is "It's *good* to be a fan." I have yet to feel like a great practitioner of anything in particular. I have a small and impractical gift set. But if there is any one thing I do feel like I'm pretty good at, it's being a fan. I am the most heart-first, passionate, deeply devoted fan of anything and anyone I love. I am such a fan of my friends, of music, books, film, the NBA, whiskey—not necessarily in that order. I am open to be astonished, to be moved, to be taken somewhere I haven't been, shown something I haven't seen. I am bad at so many things, but I succeed at fandom.

And maybe that's not such a bad thing after all.

Trusted Guides

I am owning up to this good word: it *is*, in fact, good to be a fan. Almost every good thing I have ever stumbled into has been connected to being a fan, to finding the voice of the stranger in all kinds of strange company. There is something about walking with the stranger on the Emmaus road that opens the two disciples up, that broadens them, expands them, challenges them to read the texts of their holy book differently, to read the texts of their own lives and experiences differently.

When I see the goodness, when I hear that sound, that voice ("My sheep hear my voice" [John 10:27]), I try to follow the goodness where it goes, follow it back to its source—at minimum, "stay there" for a while. If that doesn't sound empirical enough, I don't know what to tell you. Philosophical and theological ideas aren't real and can't hold you up. We need the truth embodied in the voice of the stranger. Those bread crumbs always lead us somewhere.

It is true I am an awfully big fan of some people who happen to be followers of Jesus. That's not because I don't believe there is any other goodness in this world; it's just that despite whatever evidence there may be to the contrary, it has been through the story of Jesus that the goodness has found me, and within that story that I have found myself.

When I consider who I am a "megafan" of, I will always think of Sister Margaret Gaines, my adopted Pentecostal grandmother and faith mentor who left us in 2017 but will not leave me alone. There is a peculiar mix of tough and tender that comes together in the women from my tradition, a capacity for what feels like otherworldly softness and an impossible orneriness that defies the definition the world has handed us. Sister Margaret was such a person, called to the ministry as a nineteen-year-old from Pell City, Alabama, and denied by her denominational mission board. She went to Tunisia anyway . . . and then on to the little Palestinian village of Aboud, where she spent all of her love and all of her life. She was bold, a woman of fire, of sanctified obstinance.

There was a tenderness to Sister Margaret that sliced right through you. The first time I ever sat down across a table from her, her presence was like a fatal wound—so light and heavy with good all at once. I said then that to be with her was what I imagined it was like to be in the physical presence of Jesus, and I still believe it.

The church culture that she came from, like mine, did not have a place for Palestinians, arguably the most in-between, ambiguous people in the world today. But they became her people, Aboud became her town, and as a Christian woman from the southeastern United States, she lived the most authentic life of peacemaking I have ever seen with her Muslim neighbors. She told me once that "if you walk in the Spirit of God, the Spirit will dissolve the acidity of any violent spirit that comes against you," and I believed her.

"Oh, if every village had a living, breathing Spirit of Christ walking in their midst, they would have a lot more peace." —Sister Margaret Gaines

Like any true saint, she was deeply humble, and was uncomfortable with anyone making too much of her. She lived to make much of Jesus. I hear her soft cry in my ear even now, speaking these words: "Oh, if every village had a living, breathing Spirit of Christ walking in their midst, they would have a lot more peace." The living, breathing Spirit of peace that was in Margaret filled her with love, boldness, humility . . . and fire.

When she died, I took part in two funerals for her: one in Aboud, where I had the profound honor of officiating with my father, and one back in Pell City, Alabama. After the funeral in Alabama, I sat down in the Cracker Barrel in Pell City with my mom and dad and Dr. Rickie Moore, my former Old Testament professor. Like Sister Margaret, Rickie has always been deeply humble, a man who has spent his life immersed in the Hebrew prophets to the point that he is like one of them himself.

So we all sat together in the Cracker Barrel, feeling the wrenching absence of Sister Margaret the way those early disciples must have felt in Jerusalem after the death of Jesus. Toby Keith hymns were playing in the background. The decor looked like a Hobby Lobby reimagining of someone's memory of a photograph of a barn. I do remember for sure I was eating pancakes, because drowning myself in maple syrup is one of the things I do when I am sad.

Rickie was sitting between my father and me, and as we swapped stories of this saint's incredible life, he said something that made me halt my pancake devouring midbite: "When elders go up, mantles go down." He was referring to the Old Testament story of the prophet Elijah, taken up to heaven in a whirlwind, and the younger prophet Elisha, who was given a double portion of his mantle—his authority. And he individually asked the three of us, my mom and dad and me, "Which part of Sister Margaret's mantle do you feel called to pick up?"

I can't remember for the life of me what I said to that then. What I remember crystal clear is what Rickie said, because it was so very much like his entirely unpretentious way of being in the world: "I know what I feel called to do . . . is to sit right here," he said, gesturing to the space he occupied at the round Cracker Barrel table between us. He knew that my parents and I loved Margaret dearly and that the love we shared for her was a significant bond between us, stronger than any generational and cultural differences. And he was volunteering to sit in the space between us, because that is what prophets do. They sit in the in-between spaces, wherever they might be—sometimes between families, sometimes between communities, sometimes between enemies, sometimes between the world that is and the world to come. Where there is a chasm to be filled, they fill it, whatever awkwardness that may cause to anyone involved—which is why prophets are never going to be in vogue with the kind of either/or thinking of political parties and/or Facebook. They do not sit in the moderate, neutral, safe space *in the middle* but the space in between— the most vulnerable, volatile space, out in the open, exposed.

I don't know if I have a good answer for Rickie's question yet. I don't know how to name what I am doing, and I rarely know what I am trying to do. But I do believe that I would not be who I am without the cast of characters who have moved me along the road. I am forever better for being their fan.

The Jesus I Want to Know

There are many things I love about Rev. Otis Moss III, also known as OM3, but I know one of the things that drew me to him most was that so much of the journey for me has been trying to find a way to bring all the pieces together, to be a whole self, to have a whole faith, integrated. And that is what I love so much about what OM3 does—it is seamless. Like the Emmaus story does, he lives at all the intersections—hip hop, theology, jazz, literature, poetry, community organizing, fire, humility—and he brings it all together so smoothly and so potently. That kind of witness helps erase the false distinctions between sacred and secular not only in our experience of the world but also in ourselves.

I have made numerous pilgrimages to Trinity United Church of Christ, where OM3 is the pastor, taking over for Dr. Jeremiah Wright. For me, it was a matter of following bread crumbs to the table from which Christ was feeding me. Trinity is thick with tradition—the expression of Black worship, the cadences and tones, the organ, the saints of all ages, the rhythm of a clear liturgy that is never too constricted for improvisation.

Trinity UCC does not set out to be "multicultural." It is decidedly, decisively the Black church. There are signs all around the property that read "Unashamedly Black and Unapologetically Christian." People who know nothing of such spaces will tell you that particularity is divisive. The truth is I have never encountered a more radical welcome anywhere I've ever been than at Trinity. As it turns out, the more people are grounded in the particularity of their own story, the more welcoming they are to those outside of it, not less. The bodily, ecstatic character of the worship connects me to a past and to a tradition that is "back there." But I can't think of any place or any people more futuristic. It is wisdom from the future, even if in places like Trinity they have known it for a long time.

The church truly welcomes all and, under OM3's leadership, while continuing the historic intellectual and spiritual witness of the church, has expanded that witness to include prophetic witness and concerns not traditionally central to the Black church, extending into environmental concerns. The extent to which Trinity is able to create a sustainable, beloved community that connects with people at all stages of life is nothing short of remarkable. It is a space for the prophetic counterwitness of the church, too wild for the Protestant white liberal imagination, too political (that is, present in this world) for the evangelical imagination, too insistent on love for people who only imagine burning everything down. In short, it is space for God.

At the center of this flame, always, is the same stranger who came undercover on the road to Emmaus. OM3 had already preached all morning, and between services, on his way back to his office, I marveled at how he seemed to know everybody's name in the building. Far from being a distant figurehead, he knows and is known within the community, and I saw no distinction in how he related to anybody based on any kind of social status. Already having poured out all day, and with a Sunday evening service yet to come, he was still wearing his white preaching robe as we sat back in our chairs and he talked about the centrality of Jesus to it all.

> That's the thing about Black theology—we are Christ-centric, Jesus-centric people. There is a Jesus-centric narrative, and Jesus is central . . . one, because Jesus experiences and embodies what we deal with. For example, one of the funniest things—years ago, when the movie *The Passion of the Christ* came out, my wife and I went to see it. And everybody was like, "It was so powerful, it just made me cry!" So we went with several Black people, and everybody was like, "Well, yeah, this is a violent movie, but this is like . . . Jesus was a brother." I mean seriously—everybody was like, "This is the narrative we have shared all these years. He experienced what we experienced." So we saw the antebellum South: "Jesus knows all about our troubles." We saw what has happened in terms of police brutality with the Romans and with Jesus. So we were sitting there and saying, "Yeah, this is gory and brutal, but this is the lives of so many people." So we didn't come out with tears, saying, "Oh my gosh, I didn't know." Yeah, we knew. That's what we preach, that's what we talk about. Jesus understands this. And it's central to the liberation narrative because Jesus is so clear about having this leaning and preference for those who are marginalized and poor. That is what Howard Thurman says is the fundamental question of what Jesus is doing,

speaking for the disinherited, those who have their backs against the wall. This is the fundamental story.

I know that I don't know this Jesus from the underside, but this is the Jesus I want to know, and Otis Moss III is the kind of witness I need to learn of him. One of the reasons I can't give up on the Jesus story is precisely because it is a story that, despite all the ways it has been co-opted in coercive, oppressive, colonizing ways, is true. I am convinced that the Jesus Otis Moss III preaches and that Howard Thurman describes is, in fact, the real Jesus. To leave the Jesus story altogether, for me, would be to concede it to the very people my heroes have lived their lives in protest to. The Jesus who has been used to maintain the social order of the world as it is and to uphold the status quo quite simply is not the Jesus I believe in.

The Jesus story is the fundamental story that I have seen animating Trinity UCC, the story that I have seen in the lives of people like Sister Margaret and OM3. I want to be captured by what captured them. I have seen in them "a world I would like to live in." When I hear and see distorted visions of God, I truly do not believe those who claim them speak for God, or for me, or have any correlation whatsoever to the faith story I am caught up in. I have no judgments on anybody's soul, but I do flatly believe that people in our time who speak terribly of things of God have never heard the voice that called out to Abraham, Miriam, Deborah, Samuel, Isaiah, John on Patmos, Hildegard of Bingen, Teresa of Avila, Francis of Assisi, Frederick Douglass, Harriet Tubman, William Seymour, Martin Luther King Jr., Fannie Lou Hamer, Gustavo Gutiérrez, Sister Margaret Gaines, Rowan Williams, Otis Moss (Jr. or III), and Rachel Held Evans.

I take heart in knowing this. There are plenty who profane the name of God while claiming to speak on God's behalf. There are plenty of dissonant stories that make a terrible racket and show us a Jesus whose company we'd really rather not keep, thank you very much. But what remains is "the fundamental story" of the true Jesus, the One we want to know, and we are not obligated to give airtime or authority to anything less.

For all the things we can't control in the world, we can control who we listen to and take seriously—and these are the kinds of witnesses we can choose to shape reality for us. It really *is* good to be a fan.

6

The Moment of Recognition

AS THE SUN SETS behind them against the back-drop of the desert sky, the stranger sits. The men can feel the electricity of his presence, how the current of him fills the space between them. But the inexplicable sense of aliveness that pulses through them is not like being nervy and jangled. How is it that he can make every cell of their being feel called to attention and yet be such a non-anxious, soothing presence? How can he feel so other and yet so impossibly familiar? The men set out on the road away from God. And now this little ramshackle roadside motel, with tacky colors and musty scents, feels like home. They are still in the thick of the darkest days of their lives, and yet somehow they feel at home within themselves.

There's a bottle of wine open on the table, a basket of fresh bread in the middle, the faint howl of the desert wind behind them. There's nothing fancy about the meal, but the deep crimson wine looks decadent after a long day of walking. They have spent hours in lively conversation, so there are no words exchanged as they pull up closer to the table, just soft smiles visible around the eyes, palpable gratitude for the moment unfolding for them. In a gesture of hospitality and deference toward their obviously wise and devout new friend, they ask the stranger to say a blessing in his dialect.

When the stranger picks up the bread, Cleopas feels a tempest rise in his belly. There's something terribly familiar about the open way the man holds the bread, like a gift, the way he raises it over his head, tilting his chin back, the way the light from the candle hits his eyes as he looks toward heaven, the lilt of his accent in the poetry of the ancestors. In the prayer to the One who met Moses in the flaming bush, it is like the stranger is transported somewhere, like he transports them somewhere. It is like this meal is every meal, like it is the first Passover, the first Seder, like this bread is manna from heaven that fell from the sky just for them, like this sweet wine was trampled and pressed out of their own crushing sorrows and served before them in the chalice. While still surrounded by grief on every side, the disciples hear the words of the prayer book crackle from their childhood: "You prepare a table before me in the presence of my enemies" (Ps. 23:5).

When the stranger finishes the blessing, he pauses . . . for what feels like long enough for him to visit old Father Abraham's bosom and return to them. He looks at them knowingly and offers a little "cheers" with the glass. In the silence, Cleopas can hear his own heart beating like a drum, the only thing he can hear, as even the wind goes still as death. In the hush, the stranger breaks the bread. And when he tears the bread, he might as well be tearing glass, because everything in the room shatters. He breaks the loaf, and he breaks something in them, like the last time around the table when he broke their hearts. A flicker of familiarity.

They remember the exquisite tenderness with which those hands had touched the lepers and the little children, had touched their longing. And they remember how tenderly he handled the little boy's bag lunch, how those same callused hands broke it too, down into pieces, which became more pieces, and more pieces, and more pieces, and more pieces, until it felt like that one little boy's lunch could have fed every hungry mouth the world has ever known. And they remember when they saw his body torn in two, how that last time at the table it was just like this before they broke him down and broke him open and broke him into pieces, which became more pieces, and more pieces, and more pieces, and more pieces. Oh, God, they remember *everything*. Everything.

As he reaches out his leathered hands to give them the bread, it all comes flooding back to them. As he is giving them the pieces of the bread, he is giving them pieces of themselves back. He is giving them their memories back. They are re-membering him, and they are being re-membered. Everything in them is on fire with recognition. They know who he is, they know what this means, they know who they are. And in that burst of recognition in which everything converges—the ancient story, the Moses story, the story of their trauma, the story of the past, the story of their future—then they know: what they thought was the road away from God was actually a collision course with God. It looked like they were simply walking away from the holy city, from their community, from their tradition. It looked like, perhaps even to themselves, they were simply "on the wrong path." But God had walked with them all along, on the road away from God, in a form they did not recognize. And the road they thought was going nowhere had been going somewhere all along, going here, to *communion*. They thought they had left the temple and the God they worshiped there. It turns out the temple had followed them home.

But this begs the question, doesn't it: If God himself walks with you on the road away from God, then how can even the road away from God be the wrong path? If this is a road Jesus is unafraid to walk, who is to say it is not the right road for you?

Nothing the disciples did, other than refusing to flatly ignore the grace in the company of the stranger, prepared them for this moment. In the depth of their despair, watching the world as they had known it burn to the ground, they did the one great, true human thing—they continued. They didn't do anything more noble—than to eat. But something happened in the meal that changed everything, illuminated everything. It didn't change or erase the trauma of the past. But there was a grace of illumination in that moment, a shift in their perspective, that enabled them to see everything that had already happened from a different point of view. Communion offered them something rare on any road but especially on this one: the gift of clarity.

A Taste of Grace

I don't have this kind of clarity all the time. It's not that I don't think there is more clarity to be had—there's always more perspective, and the reason I still believe in the way of Jesus, broadly speaking, is because I think it leads there. The way of Jesus is a path that entails living with the qualities of the dying while you are still alive. It's a path of gratitude and humility, listening and paying attention, putting the needs of others above the screaming, petulant demands of your own ego. But it is a wisdom path in which there is no such thing as coming into some sort of permanent, perpetual place of clarity—in which you see it this way all the time, feel it this way all the time, know it in this unhalted way all the time.

There are people who will try to sell you a quick and easy path to this way of being in the world, and a product or system that will get you there. We call these products "pyramid schemes"—many of them happen to be religious in nature. The way you learn is to live, and to pay attention while doing so, and the path and the One who went before you to carve it will reveal themselves.

Have you ever had shimmering, shivering clarity? The knowing that is deeper than words? Maybe it's a little random when it comes—which would make sense since you definitely don't have any control over when or how the stranger comes to visit you on your journey—but I can tell you this much: clarity is a little closer when we are in proximity to death and dying. The disciples have this encounter just after the death of Christ, and the Christ they reckon with then is the One who has just walked through "the valley of the shadow of death" (Ps. 23:4 KJV). We are open to the mystery in a different way when we encounter literal death, but we are also more open to it when we experience the death of a previous community or of a future that is not to be. The disciples themselves are dealing with death on each of these levels.

There is a brutal, sometimes tender clarity that comes from death, a perspective that alters your sense of the scale and scope of things, realigns and reorders priorities, gives you access to truth you already know but don't know that you know until you are driven into it—when someone else will "take you where you do not wish to go" (John 21:18).

There is one way that might be more obvious, more apparent: whenever someone we love dies, or when we or someone we love has a brush with death, immediately we have a different sense of scale for everything—what matters, what doesn't, what seemed urgent but wasn't, what didn't seem important but really is. It is a revealing both of the essential fragility of things and of the sheer, brilliant holiness of things.

I don't claim to understand its mystery, but I know enough to know that truth lingers near the end. Death has a way of revealing ultimate things, if only we wake up to see what it is showing us.

Food You Know Not Of

When the ultimate moment of recognition comes, though, it is through the gift of the meal. The overtures of Eucharist in the meal on the road are undeniable. The disciples spent their last time with Jesus before his death at the table, and it is at the table on the road that Christ is revealed to them again. But the twist here is that they didn't go looking for a sacred meal. This was the kind of "ordinary" meal you eat because you are tired and hungry, not because you are enacting some kind of sacred ritual. As it turns out, however, the bread of heaven was looking for them.

A friend on the pastoral staff at my former church in Charlotte told me a story from their college and young adult ministry, which had its own weekly service to worship and celebrate the Eucharist together. One night as my friend was leading communion, he noticed a new young man sitting at the end of the first row. When he gave the invitation to come to the table, the man did not move—he put his head in his hands and cried.

My friend's heart broke for this man. He walked over and sat down beside him, while everyone else now was in the communion line, and whispered a personal invitation in his ear. "Hey? How would you feel about going to the table with me? Could you and I go together?" The young man cried harder. "I just don't think I can. I'm not ready. I can't do it." It was as if the weight of some secret shame pinned him to his seat.

My friend's own eyes filled with tears, and he whispered something else in his ear that I will never forget: "If you're not going to receive Christ's body, I don't want to go either."

Go back and read that sentence again slower. I don't know how much more of the heart of the Christian gospel could be occupied inside a single sentence. It is the very essence of the book of Romans, in the words of my friend Chris, that "God would rather not be God than be God without us." That is the message of Christ on the cross, which is really the only thing God was ever really trying to say: "I'd rather be in hell than have a heaven without you."

My friend felt prompted by the Spirit to pray that since this young man did not feel that he could come to the table of the Lord, "God, I ask that you would bring the table of the Lord to him." He assumed his prayer was a kind of metaphor—asking that God would send the man some spiritual nourishment for wherever he was on the road. As soon as those words left his mouth, though, he looked up to see one of the people who had been serving communion standing over the two of them holding the bread in one hand and the cup in the other. He knelt down and said to the young man, "While I was serving the elements, the Lord told me to leave the altar and come bring communion to you." The young man wept, and ate.

This story reminds me so much of the story from Luke 24, because the young man opened his eyes, looked up—and there was literally someone holding the elements there in front of him. This is my prayer even while you are reading this now—that God would bring the table to you.

The Open Table

Why is it that so much weight falls in the text on this simple, elemental Last Supper Jesus shares with his disciples? While on the road, why is it that this moment of recognition does not come until *during the meal*? It is as if the entire road—as if every road, in a way—leads to the meal. There is something about the meal, the eating and drinking that Christians will come to call *Eucharist*, "giving thanks," receiving the broken body and being received, drinking of the common cup as one people. It is not just the physical bread and wine that nourish us but a restoration of the sense of community we feel we once lost, the belonging we long for—the communion not just with Christ but with one another.

I feel like I have been going on for much of my adult life about this meal. I believe in its mystery. I don't believe it is crude magic. I know that not everybody who partakes of this feast receives some kind of miraculous healing (although I believe people who tell me they have), and I have no theories about or real interest whatsoever in the metaphysics of how the meal of grace actually works.

The New Testament never seems to make it a foot without a reference to the meal. The earliest followers of Jesus weren't just in the temple but "broke bread from house to house" (Acts 2:46 KJV), which means this meal. When the apostle Paul is on a ship that is about to wreck, he breaks bread and serves a meal for everyone on board using the same language Luke, the writer of Luke-Acts, uses elsewhere for this communion or Eucharist. Suffice it to say, everywhere you look in the pages of the sacred text, there is a meal—including the end, where the story culminates with the marriage supper of the Lamb. This works out, since meals mark every significant moment of our lives most of the time really.

The mystery at the center of all things is a meal. You cannot comprehend it; you can only taste it. All the existential questions come down not to answers but to bread and wine. To anybody looking for apologetics I don't really believe in, I could give this one "bread crumb": while all major religions rightly claim, on some level, that God can be known through nature, reason, and experience, I love the particular claim that

Christ is known through eating and drinking. I love that Jesus is the God whose crumbs get beneath our tongues. I love that the body of God is given to satiate our deepest hunger. It has been said that Christians are "people of the book." Okay, I really like books—but you can still starve to death while reading them. The community that emerged around Jesus of Nazareth valued words plenty, but they were clearly first and foremost "people of the bread."

Jesus is the God whose crumbs get beneath our tongues.

Maybe you started walking because your former community was fencing the table. Maybe you or someone you cared about was fenced out. In any case, the discovery of the road is that the table Christ spreads is radically open. If death brings clarity, then it's worth noting how Jesus spreads the table when he is preparing for his own: it is the feast to which Judas the Christ-betrayer and Peter the Christ-denier are both invited. But in the same way that all of Jesus's life was in the shape of his death on the cross—nonviolent, self-sacrificial—Jesus's "last" supper was in the shape of all of his suppers. The table practice of the church finds its origin in the table practice of Jesus: "Why does your teacher eat with tax collectors and sinners?" (Matt. 9:11). I believe the Gospels, written later than the Epistles, emphasize the scandal of Jesus's table practice—which is to say, eating with everyone indiscriminately!—precisely because it was intended to shape the table practice of the early Christians. The fact that the people who claim to follow Jesus have so often not shared the central defining practice of the One they claim to worship is the primary reason Christianity—both historically and currently—so often doesn't resemble Christ.

Just as Jesus said, "Those who are well have no need of a physician, but those who are sick" (Matt. 9:12), it is simply the hungry who are in need of the Eucharist. There is no other requirement for coming to the table.

No one is morally "worthy" of the body and blood of Christ, so no one is unworthy to come to his feast! But Paul writes that we can come "in an unworthy manner" (1 Cor. 11:27). His critique of the Corinthians was not that they were unworthy people but that they came to the table in an unworthy way—turning the table of unity into a table of division. If the church underwrites the class divisions of the world, the Founder of the church will judge us, for *that* is coming in an unworthy manner. That said, coming to the table is intended to be in and of itself an act of repentance: if you are humble and hungry, you are eligible. The table brings healing, hope, and cleansing. The invitation to the table—as John Wesley rightly understood—can and should be synonymous with the invitation to salvation!

If you want God, if you hunger for God and for belonging, coming to the table *is* the way you say yes—from wherever you are or wherever you have been. Communion is *not* merely symbolic. The real presence of Christ is mediated to us through this mystery meal—though we have no idea *how* it works. If you want to know Jesus, the invitation is not "come and pray a prayer" but "*taste* and see that the LORD is good!" (Ps. 34:8).

The invitation is not just to *think* differently about him. It's more visceral, more bodily than that. Put the chalice to your lips. As we sang in the Pentecostal church, "Come and dine, the master calleth come and dine! You may feast at Jesus's table all the time!" Or we could put it this way: "The Spirit and the bride say, 'Come.' And let everyone who hears say, 'Come.' And let everyone who is thirsty come" (Rev. 22:17). The table of Christ is spread not for the righteous but for those who are hungry and thirsty for righteousness! If you want God—you shall be filled. We are offered not a new way of thinking but an actual bellyful of God!

The grace of God is such that a feast will find you, even as you walk away. When we cannot bring ourselves to come to the table of Christ, God brings the elements to us—even on this treacherous road.

A Way of Saying Yes

But what is communion precisely, anyway? The chemical properties of any kind of bread or wine can be only so different. Which exact elements count as the bread of heaven and the cup of salvation? How would you quantify such a thing? How would you know?

I love the way the Eucharist is consecrated in the Orthodox, Catholic, and Anglican traditions. I love the amount of time and energy they spend consecrating the elements—even have a certain appreciation for the rigidity of the rules around how the meal is prepared and consecrated—because it speaks of loving attention. There is so much in the tale on the road that speaks of the power of paying attention as a spiritual practice— that leads to a moment of "seeing" the stranger for who he is, in the meal. But alas, call it low church, call it whatever—I fairly stubbornly refuse to impose much of any concrete parameters on what can or cannot be communion. I think it is perfectly fine for a community to agree on a set of practices for how they are going to prepare and receive the meal. But as with Jesus turning the water into wine, if there is a miracle that is going to happen here, that is ultimately God's job and God's business. And God will do what God will do.

During the pandemic, I observed with some fascination the debates people were having over what could or could not count as communion. When people are not able to leave their homes out of concern for the welfare of their vulnerable neighbors or themselves, are they unable to take communion? The Eucharist is a shared meal, and the power of it is every bit as much in the humans we share it with as in the transaction with the divine. In fact, much of the possibility of what can happen between us and God seems to be contingent on these human connections, which is why Paul is so insistent that the exclusive, elitist, class-conscious table practice of some of the Corinthians is not merely a problem that they have with one another but a problem that they have with God.

I knew people who made perfectly eloquent arguments about how since the Eucharist is a meal that can only be shared, instead of empowering people to take elements at home in some form of online communion, we should allow ourselves to miss the Eucharist, grieve not being able to take of it together, allow our restlessness and affection for it to grow until the time we would be able to gather—essentially feel how special it is by its absence. There is a way of putting this that sounds artful. But I cannot buy it.

I can't buy it because of a story my old friend J. C. told me about growing up in Honduras. When he was fourteen, he was part of a violent street gang that was causing havoc in his neighborhood. They especially antagonized a local Pentecostal church. One night when the church was having a prayer meeting, J. C. and his friends walked to the church, put a padlock on the front door while people were still inside praying, poured a trench of gasoline around the building—and attempted to set it on fire. To their shock, none of their matches or lighters would work . . . they were unable to *set gasoline on fire*. It badly spooked him.

Over the next few months, the woman who ran the youth ministry at the church kept trying to befriend J. C. He was cynical, but something about the consistency of her kindness wore him down. She invited him to come on a youth retreat, though he wasn't quite sure what would be happening there. Being fourteen and not having anything better to do that weekend, he eventually relented and told her he would go.

When he got to the retreat, he was miserable. The head of the rival street gang, his archenemy, had experienced some kind of radical conversion and on Friday night gave a testimony to the group about how the goodness of God had changed his life. J. C. didn't know what to do with it. More than that, what really made him angry was that he didn't know all the teenagers on the retreat were following an enforced fast all weekend—they literally didn't serve any food! (Pentecostals in that part of the world don't play.) So in addition to feeling overstimulated, overwhelmed, and out of place, J. C. spent the weekend in various stages of increasingly hangry rage. He couldn't wait to get home.

The final service of the three-day retreat was on Sunday morning, which was traditionally when they would take communion. But they also were quite rigid on who could and could not receive the sacred meal—you had to be baptized in order to partake. After being bitter and discontent all weekend, J. C. said he was overcome by a strange desire to share in the meal with the other kids. He yearned for it—longed for it. He was suddenly heartbroken not to be able to eat and drink. He says to this day he has no idea what made him think to do this outside of some sort of pure desperation, but while the other kids ate their little communion wafer, he mimed putting an invisible wafer to his own lips, as if he were eating along with them. When the other kids were drinking from their little communion cups, he put an invisible cup to his own lips and mimed drinking from it. When he did, he felt something happen in his body. And about forty minutes later, he woke up flat on his back on the floor, speaking in an ecstatic language he had never learned before, crying and rejoicing—while a group of the students surrounded him praising God and praying for him.

I love this story for so many reasons, not least of which is that it defies theological convention. J. C. had not been baptized and had prayed no prayer "asking Jesus into his heart." And what precisely are the metaphysics of a mimed, invisible communion? And who exactly would have ecclesiological jurisdiction over such elements?

For me, it underscores that the table is the table of Christ, and he alone is exclusively in charge of the guest list. It's his table, not ours. Yes, there was an intention on J. C.'s part, a kind of expectation—but the mechanics of the meal were so random that there's nothing clear I know to say about it except it was his way of saying yes to God.

The table is the table of Christ, and he alone is exclusively in charge of the guest list. It's his table, not ours.

Can there even be a wrong way to say yes to God? And if God can be encountered that way through an invisible meal, then is there any meal you suppose God would not be willing to meet you in?

We don't have to get hung up on the metaphysics of this meal in order to receive the invitation, which is simply this: if you find yourself hungry on your way, in this unending spiritual journey with all its revelations, brutalities, and everything in between, pull up a chair. Take and eat. Receive the gift that Christ always extends to you at the table that is *always* open to you.

Sitting with Jesus

I believe that there is a stranger who has been walking with you down whatever road you may have taken to get to here. "Stranger," but who is familiar somehow, a presence that you know, and that knows you well. What would it be like to welcome that presence?

What would it look like to *invite* Jesus to sit down with you, the way the disciples invited the stranger? To pay attention to this with-you presence, right here, right now?

You can start by imagining your absolute favorite space in this world, the space where you feel the most safe. You can imagine yourself sitting in your favorite, most comfortable chair. Settle in. Pour yourself a glass if you need to—and if it doesn't seem too far-fetched, I might even suggest pouring him a glass! J. C. wasn't afraid to imagine a cup that wasn't a cup. What would be wrong with having a cup but imagining the person?

It's been such a long journey. Take time to breathe. And as you settle into your breathing . . . pay attention. Jesus has been waiting a long time to be able to sit with you this way. Can you imagine his face? Can you see how he looks at you? Do you see even a trace of anger, wrath, bitterness, judgment on his face? Can you see the joy that the stranger takes in being in your presence?

What do you see in his eyes? Is there a message in how Jesus simply looks at you? What is he saying to you with his eyes? Take in the way he looks at you, slowly. Feel your whole self, your whole story being received.

Chances are there is something he wants to say to you. What do you hear him saying? You don't have to be a card-carrying mystic, a TV preacher, or an influencer; you don't have to have any sort of credentials at all. Just listen, inwardly. You have everything inside you that you need in order to hear him. Don't rush.

Keep listening. Listen for where you feel the *shimmering, shivering* knowing.

Whiskey You Know Not Of

There was a bakery called Nova's in my hometown of Charlotte that came to be synonymous with being in the presence of God. I used to ride my bike there in the morning before daybreak, connect to Wi-Fi (where the password was "freshbreaddaily"), settle in, and receive my actual daily bread. I accidentally discovered that was where the Spirit showed up most reliably for me. It was where I could be reminded of the truth that God provides, that there is, in fact, daily bread that is given, that there will always be enough. The simple blessing I say over most meals started spontaneously there: "The gift of this food, and the grace of this food," because

I came to trust the reliability, the constant, of grace in that taste.

When I left Charlotte, which was the known universe to me, that always felt like a place to go home to.

When I went home a while back and found out they were closing after twenty-six years, it was unsettling. It was a time when the world in general and my life in particular felt violent, chaotic—and that portal of grace being closed felt ominous, like a way of saying maybe there would be no more grace, no more provision for me. I went there for one final morning before they closed. It reminded me of the Israelites picking up manna off the ground, having no idea where they might find bread tomorrow. Then again, when have we ever known tomorrow would be given, much less had an advance on tomorrow's grace? It was always only this day's bread—there has never been a prayer for future bread. I ate my last little meal there reverently, remembering. Inside, I was stacking my stones to build a kind of altar, grateful for all the ways Love had met me there. I remember specifically having a sense somehow of Spirit wanting me to keep my eyes open: there is always provision; there is always more.

I last visited Nova's at a time in my life that felt like perpetual famine, when I feared there would not be enough for me. Heading home, trying to unwind my mind, I swung by a local store to see if they had any bourbons to bring back that I hadn't tried. (While I appreciate the way Christ appears to the disciples through the bread and wine, I much prefer the slow, sensory delights of bourbon over wine.) It was in the middle of the pandemic, so I popped on my mask before swinging the door open.

I picked up a bottle of twelve-year-old Knob Creek Rye, a bottle I will never forget. I think it was $70, but I didn't buy it—I was just holding it, admiring it really. The cashier flagged me down and said, "Sir, someone else just bought that bottle for you. Enjoy." I was too stunned to know what to say. And then a man who was standing beside me nodded at me and said, "We don't have a lot of white folks around here willing to do that. I just want you to know I really appreciate your mask," and kept walking.

I was wearing a mask that read "Black Lives Matter," which for me was simply a basic affirmation of something unshakably true that had also come under fire in my town in Oklahoma.

I keep that empty bottle near me when I work the way other people would keep some explicitly religious artifact—because every time I look at it, I remember that God provides. As to exceptional whiskeys, Joseph Magnus Cigar Blend, Old Carter, and Michter's 10-Year Rye were so alive and rich that I've never forgotten what they tasted like in my mouth. But that bottle of Knob Creek was the taste of grace, and nothing else has ever been that good.

Jesus once said, "I have food to eat you know nothing about" (John 4:32 MSG). He apparently has some good bottles put back that I don't know about either.

I'll Have What You're Having

Bourbon, of course, is not the point, any more than bread or wine is—since apparently God is perfectly content to get to us not only where there are no glasses and no plates but also where there are no elements whatsoever. In other words, God will meet you where you are. Even when it feels like you are walking on a road with no provision, God will come to *you*, bringing the elements along.

The practice of receiving the Eucharist as part of a community is a critical part of my life I couldn't imagine living without. I highly recommend going to a community to share in a meal with God. But more than anything, I believe God is interested in sharing a meal with you. Sometimes it is not us responding to the initiative of a priest. It is Love coming as a stranger in our kitchen, asking *us*, "What's for dinner?"

Or maybe you sit down with the stranger at a restaurant, and the waiter asks, "What will it be?" looking at the mystery guest first.

The guest looks over at you, grinning. "I'll have what you're having," God replies.

7

People of the Burning Heart

SO FINALLY, that glorious moment of illumination has come. God had been walking with the disciples on the road away from God all along, but they did not know it! They were never abandoned. They were never alone. In the absolute darkest, most godforsaken moment, God was with them. They simply did not yet have the gift of recognition.

Now, in the eating of the meal, it has all come together, and as it happens in such moments, those very rare moments of absolute clarity, we just know that there is no going back to seeing the way they did before. And then, as if this bizarre story doesn't have enough plot twists already, we're hit with yet another one.

For precisely at the moment when the disciples recognize Jesus for who he is, when they are ready to reach out their arms and physically grasp the mystery for themselves—to hold it, to touch it, to handle it, to be held by it—*poof*! He is gone. The very moment they recognize the divine is the moment the divine vanishes from their sight.

It seems counterintuitive. Surely this is an inaugural event. Surely this is only the beginning, the first of many such appearances. Now Jesus is going to start following them around like Obi-Wan Kenobi, and they're not going to be able to get rid of him.

There is never a revelation so intense that every moment of life is going to feel entirely lit up in the wake of it.

But it doesn't really work out that way. Resurrection is a way of seeing the world, partly as it truly is and partly as it one day will be. But it doesn't always "fix" everything. The clarity isn't there forever. There is never a revelation so intense that every moment of life is going to feel entirely lit up in the wake of it. We are not always going to feel that kind of illumination. The fact that you don't live in this heightened state of consciousness forever does not mean that you are doing something wrong. Our conscious awareness of the presence of God comes and goes, even though the presence actually never leaves us. This pattern, almost of hide-and-seek, is the very nature of the spiritual life, and no one outgrows it.

We will not always have this kind of clarity. But we can remember what it felt like when we did and lean into this spiritual practice of remembering, against all the forces that converge to make us forget.

Pay Attention to the Flame

It is a strange reality of the spiritual life that we may be initiated into the mystery with miracles but aren't often sustained by them. This could lead to questioning the reality of God or the reliability of ourselves, and along the way, we will surely do both—but I don't know that either is necessary. It can't be that the only possible conclusions are either that God has not ever really revealed himself, that it was all a lie or a delusion or all in your head, or that there is something wrong with you that you aren't able to manufacture the magic over and over again and keep it up. That's just not how God works, not how grace works—not how the world works.

We are given appetizers of the world that is coming . . . tastes of what it could be to experience a reality in which there is no distinction between the world we see and the invisible world we don't see. It's the culmination of the story of Scripture—no distinction between the new heaven and the new earth, the good reign of God spilled fully into the realm of us, the culmination of "Thy kingdom come, Thy will be done in earth, as it is in heaven" (Matt. 6:10 KJV). It is what the prophet Habakkuk saw when he was intoxicated with a vision of the world in which "the earth will be filled with the knowledge of the glory of the LORD, as the waters cover the sea" (Hab. 2:14). Inevitably, there will be some crossover between these realities now where these realms overlap, where we experience a "thin place," where the barrier between them is papery.

But the glory invariably comes and goes. The fact that the glory is not always tangibly present does not mean the glory was not ever with us or that it will not be present with us again. This is seen in Paul's dizzying, almost braggadocious contrast between himself and Moses in 2 Corinthians 3: Moses put a veil over his face not to shield the people from the bright shininess of God's glory but to keep them from knowing that the glory came and went—compared to his own more tattered, vulnerable witness.[1] Paul says we are allowed to see the glory of God through our "unveiled faces" (v. 18)—which is a way of saying we can see the glory through the sometimes unsightly image of a person who comes in and out of the "glow."

Seamless, unbroken experience of perpetual new heights is the life sold by snake oil salesmen, not the life of the saints. Those who are marked by the divine presence do not constantly live in the awareness of God's presence—they are just forever haunted by it. The physical, corporeal, material, graspable God-in-flesh was available to the disciples only for a moment. But that is not to say that when the bodily Jesus vanished, they were left with nothing. You can put out a fire, but embers are left—there is charred, smoky wood in the aftermath, evidence of the flame, like the charred barrels of an especially smoky whiskey. The disciples could not reach out and touch the naked flame, but a kind of fire was left burning in them: "Were not our hearts burning within us while he was talking to us on the road, while he was opening the scriptures to us?" (Luke 24:32).

"Were not our hearts burning within us . . . ?" You know enough to know that when you hear words like these, this is not merely a religious matter. As if there could be any distinction between sacred and secular in the things that burn hot in your soul. As if it could be contained by language, category, words.

"Were not our hearts burning within us . . . while he was opening the scriptures to us?" also names something desperately important—that before they had the full revelation of the stranger before them, they did know something. They didn't know who he was. They didn't know what the burning meant. They didn't know where this road was taking them anymore. But they knew the road lit up differently in the light of the stranger, that the light they saw in him made them see everything else differently than they ever had before. Their hearts burned *before* they knew the identity of the man to whom they were talking. They didn't have clarity yet, but they had an instinct—they had a fire in their bellies they could not help but listen to.

Maybe this is where this whole thing goes off the rails. Is there no greater lesson here than to listen to your own yearning? Can't we burn with "strange fire"?

Fire can keep you warm, but it is hardly positive if it burns in a forest, as we learned from that wise guide Smokey the Bear. Is the point that all burning is good? Hardly. There are things that burn toward destruction and death, not light and life. Rage burns. Revenge burns. Pure animal lust burns. But is that what burns in the inner chamber, in the depths of you? What the two disciples heard from Jesus didn't just make their skin tingle—it made their hearts burn.

It is here I must put in a word for that flame of love we call the Holy Spirit that came to rest on each of Jesus's apostles. Jesus said he would not leave us alone but would send another comforter—and that presence that would descend on us would be the same fire that raged in the burning bush but did not consume it.

The flame of the Spirit may burn everything in us, but it does not destroy us.

That is how we know this fire apart from all the others: it may burn everything in us, but it does not destroy us. This fire, unlike my fire, purges, purifies, and refines, but it does not annihilate. For those of us who read every reference in Scripture to "fire" as if God's fire is like our own, we would do well to consider that the flame of God cannot and should not look like the flame of Satan—the flame of accusation, of blame, of its most dangerous simulation: rightness. If we can tell no difference between the flame of love and the flame of the devil, we won't know the difference between the fire that creates space for new life and the fire that destroys everything that lives already. We won't be able to tell the difference between arson and refiner's fire.[2]

But what about the things that linger in the deepest part of you when the meal is over and the night is growing old? Is there nothing to the things that are yet burning within you? Is there within the embers no evidence that God has been here? The flames are not merely a memory of where Christ has been. Flames are the future. When the day of Pentecost fully came, tongues of fire rested on each of them—everybody had their own, but each flame came from the same Spirit.

The flame of the Spirit is always present. It becomes our work to *remember* the fire. It becomes our practice to *pay attention* to its brilliant blazing.

When Was the Last Time You Felt Your Heart Burn?

We may listen to our top-level, superficial desires far too much, but we listen to our deepest desires far too little. If your way of discerning the truth within you is detached, cerebral, intellectual, over-against-your-body, some sort of Western, scientific, Enlightenment rationalism—well, you enjoy that (to the extent that people living in denial of their deepest selves actually enjoy things). But the fact is that revelation comes in a way that interrupts all those cold ways of knowing . . . however briefly. Thankfully, the disciples didn't debunk this firsthand, sensory, sensual, experiential way of knowing but instead could not deny their own inner witness: "Did not our hearts burn within us?" (Luke 24:32 ESV).

The disciples had been through trauma, were headlong down a long trail of grief. They had many reasons to want to believe in a magical, hopeful story—maybe even reason enough to generate one if none existed. In the Hebrew Bible, there is a story in which Elijah the prophet squares off against the false prophets, each asking their God or god to bring down fire upon an altar. The false prophets are all noise and activity—they work themselves into a frenzy. They act as if something extraordinary is happening even if it is not. But when Elijah prays a short prayer, the fire falls. There is a kind of fire that no mere human can start and no mere human can put out.

But you say you don't believe in fairy tales like the resurrection or prophets calling fire from the sky—or at least you don't believe that such things happen in your life. You say you have met no magical strangers on the road, unveiling the secrets of life and death. Okay. Well, tell me this, friend—when was the last time you felt your heart burn? The last time you felt spiritually alive? Even if there is some dust and miles and memory between you and that moment, some part of you remembers—and some part of you knows. Didn't your heart burn within you then?

Was there a *shimmering, shivering* knowing?

A Different Kind of Fire

When somebody cuts me off on the interstate, that is one kind of fire. When my ego is wounded, I feel slighted, overlooked, inconvenienced—that is one kind of fire. It's petty fire, small but destructive—ultimately uninteresting. You have to feel a lot of things along the road, and sometimes anger or rage can get you out of the driveway toward some place you need to go—but it will take you only so far. When you are trying to figure out what sort of fire is within you, ask, "Where would this fire take me? Does it consume/destroy, or could it yet create?"

I would need a whole separate book to tell you about how, after listening to the voices of friends and other people of faith who don't look like me, who gave me an account of a different reality than the one I swam in, this new reality caught fire in me. What I can tell you in short is that I came to be convinced that the people from whom I learned these things were holy people, and this was holy fire, not to simply burn the world down but to transfigure it—the way the flames of Pentecost do.

When the day of Pentecost had fully come, flames of fire "rested on each of them" (Acts 2:3). There is a particular flame that sits on you, that rests on you—a fire that is now in you. It is not meant to be ignored or quenched but welcomed, cultivated. You were not designed to smolder but to burn.

It is the great gift I was given growing up in the tradition I did—an appreciation for and an active cultivation of the fire. I can't leave it alone, or at least it won't leave me alone. The following meditation came from a deep place in me, as this is the Pentecostal understanding of the Spirit—the experience of God as "a burning fire shut up in my bones" (Jer. 20:9).

> I love the uptown church and the cleric with
>   the collar
> but my faith came up from the mill and from
>   the holler
> fiery lady preacher said yes when she heard
>   God call her
> the wrong side of the tracks, where the road
>   isn't calmer
>
> I believe in fire.
> I believe in fire.
> I believe in fire.
>
> while y'all were in school we freaked out in the
>   schoolhouse
> shouting out our faith and shouting through
>   our doubts
> preacher never said to be quiet like a church
>   mouse
> Sunday isn't over 'til you sweat through suit and
>   blouse
>
> I believe in fire.
> I believe in fire.
> I believe in fire.

the wild faith that grows in the open country
   meadow
is the wild faith that grows in the skyline
   shadow
is the faith that rebels against the claims of the
   pharaoh
in a God big enough to keep his eye on the
   sparrow

I believe in fire.
I believe in fire.
I believe in fire.

they keep us making bricks or they keep us
   plowing
we are told to keep the peace, there's no need
   for shouting
don't break the concentration of the rich man
   counting
I see the golden statue, but we didn't come for
   bowing

I believe in fire.
I believe in fire.
I believe in fire.

it's all right if you don't understand the music
   or the fuss
if you really have to call it, call it cantankerous
it doesn't really matter what you decide to
   name us
so long as you know . . . you're not going to
   tame us

I believe in fire.
I believe in fire.
I believe in fire.

prayers and protests are born out of insistence
caesars and czars will not stop this resistance
tongues and dancing are wartime instruments
beware the sound of sanctified dissidence

I believe in fire.
I believe in fire.
I believe in fire.

from the red glow, in the shadow of the empire
our salty sweat incense rises higher and higher
come all you misfits all you dreamers all you
    liars
you can quench the Holy Ghost, but you
    cannot deny her

I believe in fire.
I believe in fire.
I believe in fire.[3]

Look Closer

Where does your heart burn? When did your heart
burn last, and why? I am not saying that whatever your
heart burns for is what you are supposed to do, in the
way you may have thought about doing it. I am aware
that sometimes we can burn for things and realize later
that there was something misguided, misplaced about
the fire, or that the fire wasn't about what we thought

it was about. That's why discernment, prayer, and conversations with spiritual friends are so valuable. I still think that usually when we've just been distracted by the fireworks or flash, that's not the same thing as Pentecost fire. Superficial desire to be successful or famous, ego need, is not Pentecost fire.

The invitation is to pay attention to whatever burns within you. You just have to pay a little bit more attention, not less . . . to look closer, listen closer to the inner burning—to what makes you more alive. If you let this part of yourself die, this essential fire that is animated by Spirit, it is not just your own life that will suffer but the lives of the people you love and who need the warmth of the flame in you. The Spirit is poured out on us so that we might ignite the flame in others.

Burning for the Scriptures

It is significant for us that it is at the moment when Jesus "opens up the scriptures" that their hearts begin to burn. Because for many of us, that is not our knee-jerk response to this particular book, not after all the ways its misinterpreted teachings have hurt us. I know a lot of people are deeply disenchanted with these very texts, and I understand that—because people have read them flatly, woodenly, without imagination, insight, or understanding. But I do not see the situation as "primitive people gave us a primitive text with problematic things that we should have all outgrown by now." I see it as a tradition of faith that gives us a multitude of voices within the canon, with full awareness that there is violence in some places and mercy in others, with no expectation of it being read outside a faithful community that grapples with the text.

The disciples, however, had a teacher, someone along the road who illuminated the words in a way they had not seen—brought out some things they had missed, surely minimized other things they had once thought were crucial. For them, the revelation was not in the scroll but the man who revealed the truth of the scroll to them—and then every word could be made sense of only in light of who he was, what he said, what he did; their experience of this living, breathing Christ relativized everything they thought they understood about the story before. Because now that it was clear that the story was always about him, and in him, and that he contained all of their stories, they needed a very different way of reading the texts they assumed they knew. The person of Christ met them on the very road on which they were walking away from the texts that had lost life for them. If you have been wounded by misreadings of the Bible, could you imagine a mending presence coming to you through the very words that were once weaponized against you?

There are people who assume that a story like this one is in the past tense, a historical account of how these two disciples came to interpret sacred words. They assume that we have the resources through some combination of history, tradition, and pseudoscience to make sense of them ourselves, without having such a teacher. Over against those assumptions, I maintain that the words are not life until the resurrected One breathes life into them along our own journey in a way that is firsthand, personal, experiential. In a way that will leave our hearts burning, in a way that will often leave us with more questions than answers.

Why I Stay with the Story

One of the people in my life who most marked me by their fire for Scripture was my friend Rachel Held Evans. We started writing around the same time—but I was decidedly her fan, and will always be. She had a way of dancing and wrangling with the text that was both reverent and playful.

She didn't have any institutional support or structures to prop her up; she was just smarter and scrappier than anybody else. Yet like all the saints I have known, she had a cocktail of fierceness and tenderness. A relationship of mutual admiration and respect became a wonderful friendship, and she did for me the same thing that she did for so many others: created space. People who were not a people became a people. I like to say it was like all these disparate characters were written into some Southern gothic novel. And she actually did "write us in"—into the gospel story her very life embodied. And that circle is ever widening, ever expanding, even now. She gave us the resources to reclaim our faith from the forces who said we had no place in it. Rachel wrestled for that reclaiming . . . for all of us.

She wouldn't let anybody take Jesus from her, take her Bible from her. She didn't run away from the angry religious mob or from difficult texts. She was willing to fight for her faith; she was willing to fight for all of us.

Even now, I can still taste the leftover spaghetti casserole we ate at her kitchen table for lunch after I made a perfect drive into East Tennessee. I was getting ready to leave the apartment I had rented for a brief season in Nashville and wanted to go back out to see her and Dan and the kids in Dayton. What was supposed to be a couple of hours turned into the longest, most leisurely, magical day. Her last book was her book on Scripture, *Inspired*, and we talked for hours about the things that had been surprising us, shocking us, and perplexing us within the Scriptures.

We recorded some of the conversation in her basement that afternoon, which barely happened because I am inept in every way. I couldn't get my own camera working—but her husband, Dan, of course had it going within minutes. The footage we shot that day of us laughing and talking theology is among my greatest treasures now.

There is no way we could have known then what trauma and tragedy the months ahead were going to bring—that this would be the last time I would see her on this side of the veil. But in the way of last things, every contour of that day is burned into my memory now, the delight and the sorrow all feel like a mandate.

We were actually talking that day about wrestling with the texts, staying in the ring with them, like Jacob wrestling the angel. "You have to demand the blessing," she said. "I'm going to wrestle with you until I get a blessing. And there are a lot of texts, a lot of biblical stories—from Hebrew Scripture all the way up through the New Testament—where I have yet to get my blessing. But I'm not giving up. There's still a lot that doesn't make sense to me or that troubles me, or that has been used and abused in violent and demeaning ways, where it's really hard to see any redemption in them. Those are still there for me. But I just can't give up."

"Why don't you think you can give up?" I asked.

"This is the question too—why are you still a Christian? First of all, it's just Jesus. The story of Jesus is the story I'm willing to risk being wrong about. That's how I answer whenever anybody asks me why I'm still a Christian. I know I could be wrong; I know I could have all of this wrong. But there is just something about Jesus that remains so compelling I'm willing to take the risk of faith. That's why I can't give up on it."[4]

Her statement is infinitely more compelling to me than "ten ways to prove the Bible is true without using Scripture." I don't have ways to prove that the lively, enigmatic, pulsing, bruising stories within those texts are "true." I believed in Rachel, and still do. I believe in the lives of the people who were able to stay connected to the story of faith because of her, and the ones who decided they didn't need to take their own lives because of her, for that matter. I believe in the impossible curiosity, fierceness, empathy, and blue-collar commitment to actually do the work with the words that she brought into the world. I believe in the space she created that literally did not exist before.

When Rachel passed and we were all grieving, I asked Dr. Rickie Moore's question to myself and some of my friends as a way of trying to keep my own spirits up: "What part of her mantle do you feel called to carry?" I don't believe that the death of any person has any kind of one-to-one "meaning" that could ever mitigate the pain of the here and now, and the shattering of such loss is mostly just disorienting to me. I didn't know how to answer Rickie's question that day in the Cracker Barrel days after Sister Margaret died on the heels of a long life, much less after Rachel's death on the heels of a powerful but short one. What do I know?

I only know that the conversation I had with Rachel over leftover spaghetti casserole felt good and true and holy, the kind of meal in which the conversation never feels quite done, the kind of time that makes you say, "Can you please stay here for just a little while longer?" I know that it left my heart burning long after.

When the disciples told Jesus to stay a little longer, they did not yet know the meal they were about to share would be a sacred meal—or how short their time with the mysterious stranger would actually be. They just knew enough to know that they wanted to be in the presence of this person for as long as they could.

Rachel's death seemed to break the dam to so many other sorrows in the world soon after, all of which felt much less bearable without her embodied presence, doing what she did the way only she could do it. But I do see her work and witness continuing to live on in ways that are deeper than memory, and I feel the truth of her life in a way that won't let me stop doing what I do when I don't feel like doing it. I am no closer to having any answer to why. I just believe that the Pentecost fire that burned in her should still be burning in the world. I believe in the fire in her that made me remember my own.

The Open Secret of Resurrection

Resurrection was crucial to the story Rachel believed in, just as it was crucial to the disciples on the road and their moment of burning clarity. Resurrection is the open secret on which all created things hang—not hidden but sometimes obscured by the threat of death. Believing in the resurrection is less a matter of dogma than a reality you can see for yourself, because you taste it within your own little existence. Death and resurrection are the pattern of things, the way of things, so the alleged finality of death is really and truly not the end.

The best news is that resurrection is not up to you. It's not even contingent on your believing it. It's what I love about Easter. By the time it comes around, we will have fallen off some bandwagons and jumped on to some others. But nothing stops the inevitability of rising. You got drunk or sober, married or divorced. People were born; people died. Nothing ever stops it. Our accomplishments can't speed Jesus up; your failure didn't slow him down. Love got up, in his own sweet time. Death was conquered. Maybe you don't believe it. So? What you *believe* won't make it more or less true.

Resurrection is God's responsibility. Some people today will go to church and be "strangely warmed." Some will leave still disillusioned. Either way, *the whole cosmos changed.* Easter is good news for every blade of grass, every cell and grain of sand. Life conquered death, and there's not a thing we can do about it. Receive it as a gift, doubt it, be wayward or devout—it happened and is happening. Resurrection is not an edict or a summons but an invitation to know the open secret humming beneath all created things—*death is not the end.* We try so hard to destroy Love and ourselves and exhaust all our chances—but we aren't competent enough. Praise God, we fail at ruining it all.

> We try so hard to destroy Love and ourselves and exhaust all our chances—but we aren't competent enough. Praise God, we fail at ruining it all.

If you've traveled on the road this far, you know—there is no straight line to resurrection. The world never seems to cooperate long with Easter hope. But on Easter, we glimpse the future—the inevitable glory that awaits all creation. However different the world will be or not be tomorrow, we cannot unsee what we saw today: what happened to Jesus will happen to us.

There are these moments, though, when we see it more personally, when we glimpse it for ourselves. How about you? Have you ever been broke; have you ever been broken? Have you ever lost the plot and your own true name? Have you ever felt jagged contempt for everything in the mirror? Have you ever hated yourself and the world? I have, more than once. I've been to the bottom of the well, to places too low for even demons to walk. Let me tell you what I found there.

I found the things inside that do not break when every bone of your body is broken. I went deep enough into the cold to find the undying flame. I forgave myself, then everybody else. I found, like the disciples on the road found, that what I thought was the end can never be—that God being God will always have the last word, even after death.

Have you ever felt so much fire in your bones that you could hear yourself crackle when you walked? I have—I walk like that just to go check the mail. Have you ever felt a love rise inside you so fierce that the force of it scared you? I have, and you are right to be afraid. Have you ever shared communion with every single created thing? I have, already today. I'm doing it now.

There's a fire that burns in me that I did not start and cannot stop. Call it swagger if you want—I call it Spirit. Spirit blows over me, into me, out of me—the wildness of Trinity surges out of my control.

I don't have to be faster. I don't have to be stronger. Nor do I have to pretend any longer to be less powerful than I am: I am made of the flame. God swims hot in my veins. The power is not mine—go ahead and tremble if you need to.

I hold in me the secret that slumbers beneath the graveyard—and comes raging back to life . . . shouting.

8

The Way Home

WHERE IS HOME, THEN? And is it possible to go back there? What would it even really mean to go home? We start out on the road because the sacred space is no longer a safe space. But even after we leave, homesickness is the ache that follows us along the journey.

It might have seemed unimaginable when leaving the sacred space that there would ever be a way to go back. For all the surprises along the road, maybe going back to where you started is the one thing you couldn't have imagined. But the journey that began with the disciples walking away from Jerusalem does end with them going back. It's interesting just how quickly that happens. My friend Chris muses that if they were on the journey to or toward their houses, maybe the places they had accepted as home were not in fact really places of rest for them. In the revelation of Christ on the road, they saw in him their home, and his table became the table of a new family.

"Where two or three are gathered in my name, I am there among them" (Matt. 18:20).

In their pain, two disciples became a community of three in which Christ was present. But what drove them back to their larger community was the need to share their joy. They would, in fact, return to where they came from, but they would not return the same because of the journey.

There is a way that all the great human stories come full circle—you go back home after a long journey as a very different person to a place that is not the same. There is something necessary sometimes about returning to the places that shaped us, seeing them from a different point of view. But when the two disciples got there, they "found . . . their companions gathered together" (Luke 24:33). If they finally found home in the risen Jesus, maybe going back to Jerusalem wasn't about a straight returning to a place at all . . . but going back for their people.

Maybe for you, "going home" is not returning to something you've known before but venturing out toward a new home, a new community of believers who show you a world in which you want to live. Maybe for you, it looks like finding a new spiritual community. Or maybe it is going back to the precise place that you left as an entirely different version of yourself. In this and all things, the Spirit guides you.

More Than One Way to Go Home

This road is too complex for there to be an overly neat, definitive, highly prescriptive guide to tell you how to walk it. I believe in staying alive on the road—so I believe in improvising. But there are some movements to this story that I think we are wise to attend to.

Going back to Jerusalem after they left it in disillusionment and despair fits the great pattern of every story—there is always a kind of coming full circle. Sometimes going back is not the path at all but coming full circle in the broadest, grandest sense—following the circular pattern of the story of God through life, death, and resurrection, but in a form of life that bears little resemblance to the life you had before.

Whatever it means to go home, it does not mean that we go back to being the people we were before the hope we once had died and changed us into something else. Not only is returning to who we were before not ideal, but it is also not possible. What the disciples saw in the death of Jesus was not something they could unsee. While the experience left them with wounds to be healed, healing is not denial or an undoing of the past.

It should be noted that there are different ways of going home, so that even to speak of going home is not monolithic. In Luke 2, after the boy Jesus stays at the temple to further his mission instead of going back home with his family, he still ultimately does go back home a few days later as an act of surrender. When the disciples leave Jerusalem, it is an act of resignation and defeat. These are not the same.

Some people can go back to their old town, their old house, their old community and be someone new, be who they are now. Some people cannot. There are some spaces that are too toxic, and sometimes there has simply not been sufficient time and healing yet to revisit former spaces. That is always okay. Any and all emotions are also okay. There are time and space on this road for every form of grief, anger, hurt, in their many forms, and it's not helpful to judge those feelings harshly in yourself or others.

There is a difference between merely going back and coming full circle.

What is not possible, at least for most of us, is simply to act as if none of the pain and trauma ever happened and move on. It will not work, for most of us, to never revisit, out of dread or fear, any of the places that shaped us. The disciples found a way to go back to Jerusalem with an entirely different way of seeing the world and seeing themselves—now through the prism of resurrection. They didn't avoid Jerusalem but brought the new experience they had back to it . . . when the time was right. The new story they were living had to be integrated with the old story. There is a difference between merely going back and coming full circle. The resurrection will never require you to simply "go back" to the person you were before, the places you were before, without the transfiguration that comes with its witness. Sometimes coming full circle doesn't mean going back to the old spaces at all; it means giving yourself permission to carry forward whatever things you still need from those spaces while giving yourself permission to let some other things go.

Some of the same people may be part of your story, others may not. But inevitably, to walk this kind of road is to walk toward a new community. The experience the disciples had on the road was the catalyst for them to build a new community, in some ways similar and in other ways dissimilar to the one they had before. Continuity and discontinuity with what came before are both allowed—but simply not having community, not ever being part of building something new, will erode us. We are not meant to live without community. Without any stipulations as to what that community has to look like or what form it might take, community is crucial to how we survive and flourish, even with all its risks, even when the very thing that set us on this path to begin with was a disappointment that we experienced with or in a community.

There is also this provocative insight: shared pain, shared disillusionment kept the disciples from being alone and sustained them temporarily in a way that was utterly crucial. The road is long, and we cannot enter into the reality of new life until we've had time and space to grieve the old one. I cannot stress this enough: that process should not and cannot be rushed. There is no resurrection without death. We can find solidarity that is holy and important in the grieving. If pain is the only thing we have, then pain can be the thing that holds us together with someone else who is in pain. Beautiful community comes into being all the time when people come together who are able to hold each other's hurt. Long term, though, there are things that can and must hold us together beyond the trauma of what happened.

The long-term community the disciples would form would need a broader basis than shared hurt—there would also be an element of shared joy. Community is meant to be a gathering around a common fire, a Pentecost fire, that brings warmth and light. This thing that we love, this passion that we have, this thing that we all call good, this thing that is hopeful and beautiful . . . this becomes the basis of what we are building.

It is more than okay to feel the sting of feeling cast out, driven out. But if anyone ever made you feel unwelcome in a sacred space, they do not get to now set the agenda for the rest of your life, as if every movement is somehow a reaction to them. There is permission to be new, to be part of something new, to grow something new, when the time is right.

Psalm 30:5 says, "Weeping may linger for the night, but joy comes with the morning." You may not know the night is over until there are no more tears left to cry. But joy is stubborn and will come up like an ornery weed when we have grieved long enough. There is newness. There is always, always newness. Sometimes it takes a while to come, but it comes.

What is bringing you joy now? Where do you sense even a sliver of new life now? Where is there laughter? Where do you see the potential for a new way of being in the world? Where is there newness?

Wherever you might find newness, it is meant to be shared. Where there is newness that is shared, where there is love that is shared, where there is good that is shared—there is the hope of a new community. We have all experienced communities in which people were too controlled, restrained, reserved, or uninterested for us to feel the freedom to speak of our pain. But there are also people who can only relate to you when you are broken down, beaten down, down and out. A friend will not be threatened to see you find joy, like an elder will not be threatened to see you find your voice. You need a company of friends who can celebrate what brings you joy as much as you need them to grieve with you when you grieve.

And maybe all of this sounds grand, but you're still searching, still walking, wandering maybe, looking for the place you can belong. Just because you haven't found such a community yet doesn't mean it doesn't exist—or that your willingness to share the gift of your pain or of your joy can't help usher it into being. Where is the hope of this new community based on resurrection? Wherever there are the ashes of one where hope has been lost.

I hope you have already given yourself permission to name your deepest pain along this road. Dare you speak of your hidden joy?

Worlds Colliding

When you have had a taste of resurrection, the world that was and the world that is coming start to come together. There are glimpses of how the parts of your story that might have felt disparate before somehow might begin to fit. I never valued stability that much, but there's a kind of rootedness I see sometimes in the lives of my friends that makes my own more wandering path seem ridiculous by comparison.

I don't claim self-awareness is my strong suit, and thinking too much about perception is not good for anybody. But I hear the voice in my own head sometimes: Why do you always have to do this the hard way instead of the easy way? For me, this has been a walking *to* somewhere, but the journey has taken me far enough from where I started to where I can flip it—and hear the voice that says you are a could-have-been, a might-have-been. I can hear the voice that says my own faith has evolved not as a journey to wholeness but as a tragedy. The road can take you far. You do wonder—or at least I do—how did you get from where you came from to where you are exactly?

The main reason I still self-identify as a Pentecostal Christian is that the story I was given, in which the central reality of the Spirit was my primary orientation to God in the world—lively, dynamic, interactive, fluid—is the story I still choose to live in. More simply put, I still choose to believe in all the things. Several years ago, I had a very unusual prayer experience with an older, wiser friend of mine. Over cigars and drinks by the pool at 2 a.m., he started praying for me in tongues—in a language he did not know—and all of a sudden, not just his language but also his tone and voice changed, even his eyes and face looked different in that moment. And then he began to speak words to me in English, words about how the calling on my life connected to the calling that was on my pioneer Pentecostal grandfather, words about me being a father—which landed in a tender place since, biologically, I am not.

The experience was very much one of home, from home, of bringing me home. And yet, it spoke of the ways that I never felt at home, that I so often felt in-between. He spoke with great particularity into the specificity of the weird work that I do, the weird way that I do it, and what that would mean for others in time. One of the things he said to me was that I was like the biblical character of Jonathan, my namesake, who was both King Saul's son and David's best friend—so that part of my role was to always be in the awkward, in-between spaces, between worlds, never feeling fully understood or accepted. At the time, so many things about my life were being reinvented, and I didn't know how all the pieces fit together anymore. Everything he said spoke into my past, where I had come from, the person I had been—but it also spoke into my present and future, the person I was, and was becoming, and would become. There was a sense of being gathered, of the story that has always been my story coming full circle, moving forward in a new way.

Soon after that, someone else I barely know sent me a message that said they were praying and felt impressed to tell me that they believed God was saying that, like Jonathan in the Bible, I was loyal to the King—in this case, Jesus—and it meant being called to look foolish and take the fall often before kings. In any case, it seems like looking down and being awkward are not just peripheral features but central contours of whatever it is I have for a "calling"!

Maybe that is a kind way to put it, and the more simple explanation is that I just missed it all by a country mile. But I am also willing to look again . . . and have been. Yes, I love the people and places I come from, I love Jesus, I have an appetite for the things of the Spirit that has never gone away. I look at my life and see a long, clear trajectory, a long arc that has always bent the same way. Far from being a fluke, whatever it is that I am doing is the product of my life being pushed to the same intersections over and over again.

Being at Home Where You Are

Where is home? There are some people I can't do without, and being with them feels like home to me. But as a place? I have less of a sense of that than ever. There is a very real way in which I am coming to be about as equally at home and as equally restless wherever I am. "The kingdom of God is within you," Jesus said

(Luke 17:21 KJV). I am quite fine with the idea that to be absent from the body is to be present with God (2 Cor. 5:8), but I don't think being taken off somewhere else was ever the point. Jesus told the disciples just before his crucifixion, "In my Father's house are many rooms. If it were not so, would I have told you that I am going to prepare a place for you?" (John 14:2 CSB). But where Jesus goes, then, is not off to a celestial construction site—he goes to the cross, on which he absorbs all the rejection, blame, scapegoating, and accusation that have ever been hurled at us. In taking all of our displacement, he made a place for us—in God. It is the unfathomable heart of the one Jesus calls Abba that has "many rooms," and you can abide in them wherever you are.

There is a very real way in which I am coming to be about as equally at home and as equally restless wherever I am.

There is a wholeness and completeness I carry with me wherever I am. There is a certain longing I carry with me too, because there are ways this experience of the love of God is not yet fully realized in the way it one day will be, and there is the aching absence of people whose company I miss. My friend Chris and I were talking about the disciples' journey between Jerusalem and Emmaus, and he said, "Maybe that's the pattern: we are living between two homes—one that should be ours, and one that actually is."

Our hearts burn within us as we navigate our relationship between homes, keeping us going. It is the very nature of the spiritual journey to never arrive in this life. We will never have the perfect experience of community, because as much as we are meant for each other, community is inevitably a mess given all the ways we are individually. The best "homes" have their own imperfections, but that's okay—the belonging we have in Christ is real and can be relied on. It is precisely because our capacity to annoy and wound each other is so great that we need a power beyond us to carry the ambiguities and complexities of our friends and of ourselves, and yet we can still find that there is no place like "home."

We come to the table again so that once more our eyes might be opened. Not every experience of communion feels like a miracle, where the heavens split open and every morsel of the bread seems heavy with Christ. Sometimes the meal just feels like a meal. But we remember what it felt like when our senses knew it was something more, and that time will come again. So we continue to spread the feast, knowing that when we dine at the table of Christ, we always taste the future.

9

What Had Happened on the Road

SINCE WE STARTED on the road, so much has happened! How can it all possibly be recounted? How can so sweeping a journey possibly be summed up?

As the Emmaus journey concludes, we read:

> That same hour they got up and returned to Jerusalem; and they found the eleven and their companions gathered together. They were saying, "The Lord has risen indeed, and he has appeared to Simon!" Then they told what had happened on the road, and how he had been made known to them in the breaking of the bread. (Luke 24:33–35)

I love that little phrase: when they got back to Jerusalem, they "told what had happened on the road."

Because what had happened on the road had been everything. How would you ever begin to tell everything that has happened to you on the road? And would anybody believe you if you did?

Can you still remember all that happened that sent you packing to begin with? The deaths you witnessed in the sacred space that you once thought was a safe space? All the hopes, dreams, and people you just knew you couldn't live without but you had to learn to live without anyway? Do you remember the little accidental churches that sprung up along the way as you opened up your holy grief to someone else? Do you remember all the fires you witnessed, the new flame that someone kindled in you when you thought the cold would stretch into forever?

Can you believe you've made it this far on a road this long and this difficult? Can you believe you're still here?

You just wouldn't believe . . .

You just wouldn't believe all the things I've seen on the road, all the things that have happened, are still happening. I still can't. I could never have imagined the depth of the joy, or the pain.

We were still recording in Rachel's basement that last time I was with her, but by this point, she had her baby daughter bouncing happily on her knee while she talked into the mic. I was talking to her about the ways I was seeing how she was helping people stay connected to the Jesus story just by being who she was and I said, "There's just so many people I think who are able to resonate with your work, and it is a reason to stay, it is a reason to contend. And I think it is very orthodox, is situated so clearly within the tradition."

"Yeah—I hope so," Rachel replied. "The way I see it is that the only way this work is sustainable for me is if I'm honest with people and if I'm not trying to persuade people of anything that I am not persuaded of. I mean we all have those days where the doubt is very profound and real, but I tell people that. I don't believe this all the time. There are days I don't believe a word of this. I've just found that people will stay with you, and listen to you, if they feel like you are being honest with them. You don't have to have it figured out. You don't have to be 'right.' You don't even have to have a 'brand' or a cohesive message. If you're honest and you say something in a little bit of a different way than other people have said it, then it's like, you'll find other people who resonate. And then that community kind of starts to build your voice too. People who read me, I read what they have to say—and it's the 'iron sharpening iron,' and it's really beautiful. I feel really lucky, blessed, privileged. I don't know what the right word is there, but I feel lucky to get to do this work."[1]

I feel lucky I was in Dan and Rachel's basement that day as her daughter hung on to her, having these words to hang on to now. I could not tell you how often I have replayed them, because they remind me how to be in this world. In the moments when I am discouraged or I lose the plot, these words ground me again in the truth I want to know and the kind of community I want to be a part of building—even, perhaps especially, after so much has happened. So very much has happened. Political leaders have risen and fallen, then risen again, fallen again. We ourselves have had our share of falling and rising. Allegiances have been uncovered, and hidden treasure has been excavated. Justice has been denied, and justice has been fought for and won. There is no easy way to speak of either the sweetness of the joy or the depth of the sorrow that we've swallowed, or that has swallowed us.

Not Quite Home

We are home in some ways, not home yet in others. But seeing the road after a glimpse of resurrection changes how we see everything.

The buildings at the old Church of God State Campground, which was my sacred space, the site of all our camp meetings, youth camps, and the house of my retired grandparents, have all been torn down for years, and there are no signs of any of those wonders at all now, but no signs of new life either. There are just grass and weeds and trees and . . . nothing. Only the cracked asphalt where I walked a million miles and the pond out by my grandparents' house on the back of the property remain familiar. Nothing has taken the place of the buildings, on the grounds or in the space they occupy in my soul.

I visited my parents back in Charlotte recently. I am ever grateful for all the ways they have loved and supported me, and still do. Now in their midseventies, they bought the house where they currently live for the same reason a lot of people their age do: to get into space that feels more manageable. I still dream in the house I grew up in, but they've not been there for a long time. There is always a way I feel at home with my parents, but their house now is not a home I have known—and the city has changed so much since I left it. I've accumulated more addresses, more zip codes, and more photos with U-Haul trucks and vaguely trepidatious smiles than I would care to admit. Trying to be at home in a place that is never ours is how I suppose we live much of our lives.

Seeing the road after a glimpse of resurrection changes how we see everything.

If you have lived any amount of time at all, you see ghosts all kinds of places, but maybe everywhere is a little haunted when you don't feel like you belong to a particular land. But I think that the more I have come to be at home inside, the more I am learning to bring it wherever I am. That sounds a bit more like learning a trick than I mean for it to, a bit too much like mastery. The truth is that I learned how to find a home inside largely because I went long enough without having a literal one that I felt any real connection to. I'm actually still a big fan of stability; I just haven't had a lot of it. I had to explore the landscape within for the same reason most of us started on the road at all—I simply didn't have a choice. It has just so happened that the space within, where Spirit dwells, has turned out to be much more roomy and expansive than I could have imagined it to be. Whatever the years have lacked in terms of security, being able to be more at home in my skin when my body hasn't been quite settled is turning out to have a pretty significant upside.

Maybe everywhere is a little haunted when you don't feel like you belong to a particular land.

I looked through some of the old photos at my parents' house, trying to find myself in earlier versions of my face—preaching using a yardstick for a microphone at age two, the wide-eyed wonder of early Christmases and waking up to G. I. Joe bases my dad had put together for me, the oblivious joy I had playing the drums in church when I was only five, the surprising lack of self-consciousness I had in all my middle-school outfits (a curious mixture of turtlenecks and NBA T-shirts and jerseys . . . at the same time)—in general, a whole lot of innocence. Sometimes I do get wistful for the ways I knew the world before.

But I don't exactly want to go back, especially since the journey has only increased my sense of wonder. So much has happened! Sure, there have been bleak moments, total despair, thought-I-was-over kind of moments. But my ten-pound Havanese, Stella, who just turned six, is curled up beside me while I write. I got her when she was an eight-week-old puppy. I think of all the ways that loving and being loved by my little friend kept me going when I really had no clue what direction home might be.

What all has happened to you since you set off on the road? We are just beginning to learn how to speak about religious trauma, but the truth is that most people who have been through it would not "allow" themselves to claim such dramatic language. But it is real. It is traumatic for anyone to watch their hope for the church, the world, and their place in it die right in front of them. But you have, and yet you are still here—and that is no small thing. We don't give ourselves nearly enough credit for doing what we have done: making it through.

I couldn't have imagined any of the people I have met who have been generous to share their stories with me, and to let me share some of my stories with them—and that miracle keeps on happening every day. Every time, it feels like another tiny resurrection. I certainly couldn't have imagined the new life and love and joy I have found, the people I love and who love me, right this second.

It is not that the road has not been harrowing, frightening, or disorienting, or that I don't have any fears about what lies ahead of me still. There has been plenty of doubt, self-sabotage, tragedy, shame, terror. But I also happen to be a witness to resurrection. And when you see the dead rise, even if just from seeing yourself in the bathroom mirror, it changes how you see everything else.

Look Again

Take a moment to take inventory of all that has happened. Look at all the loss, grief, and undoing you have made it through so far. Look at all the hurt and heartbreak. Now look at your story a second time from the point of view of resurrection. Since God is often telling a different story with your life than the story you think your life is telling, and a better story than the story you tell about yourself, it is worth looking again.

From one view, what would seem to be a perfectly normal and pragmatic view, what to us can seem like the only view, the disciples left the place that they came from not only in disorientation and despair but also as utter failures. They had hoped that Jesus was going to be the One who was going to restore their people to their former glory over against their oppressors, and instead he died a convict's death, gasping and bleeding, while they ran away in fear. They left the city they dreamed in, in disgrace. That objectively checks *all* the boxes for failure, doesn't it?

And yet we know now that something else was already happening, that it was not the end but the beginning— that the road wasn't taking them toward devastation but toward restoration beyond their wildest reckoning. Reality was being turned inside out. Their eyes just weren't open yet to what was already happening.

Their story is not a story of human failure but of Love conquering over death—they just couldn't see it yet because they were still living it. I believe that is true of your story too. It's difficult to see the full panorama of our stories while we are still in the midst of them. But if we were to see the full view, we'd find our stories mean so much more than we ever give them credit for in the moment.

When you know something of who the stranger on the road is, something of the trajectory of where the story is going . . . you read the whole story differently. When you know the end of the twisty, bendy thriller film, or rewatch that season of the show after the big reveal, or even retrace the steps of somebody in your life after you come to know the thing about them you could not have known before—all of a sudden, it's a whole different experience. I'm just saying: you may owe it to yourself to look a second time.

Love has walked alongside you, even as you've walked away. The plot twist is this: the hope you saw die with your own eyes is alive and walking with you—more powerful, more present than ever before. That's the big reveal, right here in your own story, even now, even after everything.

We spend so much of our lives waiting for something to happen that will change everything. For these disillusioned disciples, everything had already changed—they just didn't know it yet.

Keep Following the Voice

Death and resurrection are not a road you walk once, because they are always happening, over and over again.

You never actually stop walking. You don't find yourself off the road, just revisiting different stops along it, from different points of view.

To be a Christian, for me, is to believe that there is a story big enough for all of us to find home, even though we rarely feel at home.

Get out of the noise long enough to remember who you really are. The tide will take you out if you let it. You can give an opinion about everything the people on your news feed are talking about and never live to make anything new. Is that really what you want? Do you want to react to everything, or contribute to a world others want to live in?

It's painful when God is leading you to a place where other people who have been important on your journey cannot follow.

You only have to find your sound and how to make it. You get to be free. Nobody owns a copyright on you. Fear will make you beholden to people who have no power over you.

It's painful when God is leading you to a place where other people who have been important on your journey cannot follow. Don't judge them or judge where you've been. God was "back there" too, and still is. Don't let your heart be arrogant now. But also . . . don't stop walking.

Just keep on following the voice of Love. Don't let the louder voices into your head. Don't give in to the panic. Don't let anybody else establish the terms. The voice . . . the voice . . . the voice. You know the One whose voice is true—and that's all that matters. It's a small voice, but focus in on it. Your path is not steady—it's not a steady time. But your heart can be. Your hands can be. Don't let anyone make you cower or tremble. The Shepherd is the One who guards your heart. Let Love himself insulate you. Keep your eyes clear and your heart open. Keep walking—knowing that Love walks with you.

A Blessing for the In-Between

Wherever you are on the map, I suspect you find yourself in between one place and another—because that is the essential predicament of humanity. Whatever you think about where you are or what it all means, Jesus has a word for all us in-between pilgrims: *blessed.* I don't know precisely where you are on the road, but I hope this blessing will extend to wherever you find yourself on it:

> Blessings to the sensitive out there who can't stop feeling the brutality in the wind that settles in their bones like winter's chill. Blessings to the overstimulated, about to collapse under the weight of their own wanting. Hear the call to fall, come apart if you have to, into Spirit's sweet rest.
>
> Blessings to the ones who still feel, despite their best efforts to numb themselves, for whom the pain runs deeper than the alcohol or pornography or food or

approval can go. May Love flood every hidden corner in your soul, by surprise. May delight wash over you, uninvited.

Blessings to the ones who do not like their bodies, or their hair, or the sound of their own voices, and the ones who feel the mirror always taunts them. May you feel the gaze of holy eyes that feast on every glimpse of you, delighting in all that you are—but never wanting, never taking.

Blessings to the childless. May you feel the surprise of new life brewing in you now, conceived neither of new love nor of science—but of the ancient Love that hovers over the chaos, creating.

Blessings to the triggered, the targets of online abuse, who bravely trudge along and share their stories and their songs, even after all they've said has hollowed them out. Warrior that you are, may you find that you don't always have to play it tough, and may you find space to be still, and know—your God and yourself.

Blessings to the guilty, for whom every step is hard under their own weight. You don't have to carry it anymore. May you fall to the ground only to find that the ground of all your being is everlasting Love. May you stumble headlong into forgiveness.

Blessings to the ones who get no reprieve from the voices out there or the voices in here, to the ones who feel tormented, haunted, pulled apart by the legion. May all the other voices but the voice of Love be silenced. May Spirit's hush fall into you softly, all the way down.

Blessings to those who still feel a long way from home, who feel this road will never end, who ache to know and to be known, but are no less lonely. Blessings to the unconvinced, the don't want to be convinced, the too numb to care, the too tired to hold on. May you be held. May you be held longer. May you be held more after that.

Acknowledgments

THERE ARE SO MANY WAYS you can walk the road, but there is absolutely no way to walk it alone. In some ways you go deep into the dark by yourself to try and get some of these things, but you come out with the fingerprints of your people all over you even more. This book is a direct homage to and celebration of the people who make me want to believe and keep going. More important than their fingerprints on this book are their fingerprints on me. And, so long as I don't embarrass them, I hope those fingerprints are as visible to you through this little window as they always are to me when I look in the mirror.

I do not have words expensive enough to repay the debts I owe, but I will pay tribute for whatever that is worth:

I want to thank my friends, without whom I decidedly would not be here, plain and simple. Joel and Tosh Everson, my true soul friends—I especially would not still be here without you, and it's important to me that you know that I know this. Thank you for being safe when nothing else was. Dr. Chris Green, the best theologian I know, and an even better, more tender human. Jarrod McKenna, for always enchanting the world, helping me and everyone you know return to themselves by gifting us so freely with your own pure spirit. Steven Furtick, both my most electric and my most generous friend. The luminous Brittney Spencer, who is all joy, my partner in crime, always carving out her own space. Cathleen Falsani, with whom I share all the same patron saints—she doesn't know that she's also become one of mine. Tony Caldwell, who watches over my soul. Brian Zahnd, the person in the world whose company most makes me feel like everything is going to be okay. CeCe Jones Davis, who inspires me endlessly. Stephanie Tait, who most makes me want to be brave. Carlos Rodriguez, in whom the flame of Love burns hot enough to knock the chill off at all times. William Matthews, who always follows the sound. Malcolm du Plessis, my faithful elder. Mark Lowry, my elder brother, who always makes me happy.

I want to thank my community from The Table OKC, which has kept me afloat despite myself: the inimitable Malika Cox, prophetess and prize fighter, always keeping me laughing and dropping just the right word when I need it most; Will and Deanna James, who have become anchors for my soul; Julie and Jeff Hodgen, wise, tender, trustworthy friends; Mackenzie Bentley, the most beautiful and free spirit, always carrying me in her prayers; Jenna Frank, the official party pastor and most hospitable person of all time; Devon and Bethany Mobley, who are authentic, vulnerable, true; Jordan Jackson, the loveliest mad scientist you'll ever meet.

I want to thank my amazing literary agent, Christopher Ferebee. I want to thank my miraculous editor, Stephanie Duncan Smith—what an honor to be able to work with you a second time. I never take it for granted that you always take my words somewhere deeper and truer than any place I ever start from.

I needed some wise guides to be road pastors to me out here. I didn't ask them to be or anything, I just kind of decided they were. So Pastor Otis Moss III, Pastor Bono, Father Richard—I've had your voices in my ears in all the rockiest places; I heard the sound of my own true name. Thank you.

Ronald and Lynda Martin—I love you both and am more thankful for you than ever. I know I have been able to keep walking largely because you have loved me so well. I hope you feel how much I honor and cherish you.

Nicole Nelson—the road is good, but I'm tired of walking all the time. I'm so glad you, Kaitlyn, Ashlyn, Alexa, and Kingston are home to me. I love you.

Notes

Chapter 1 The Road Called *Godforsaken*

1. Flannery O'Connor, "Some Aspects of the Grotesque in Southern Fiction," *Mystery and Manners: Occasional Prose* (New York: Farrar, Straus & Giroux, 1969), 44.

2. Ephesians 6:12.

Chapter 3 When the Story Gets Too Small

1. Luke 2:41–50; Hebrews 4:15.

2. Phyllis Trible, *Texts of Terror: Literary-Feminist Readings of Biblical Narratives* (Philadelphia: Fortress, 1984).

Chapter 4 Your Pain Is Real

1. René Girard, *Job: The Victim of His People* (Stanford: Stanford University Press, 1987).

2. Jonathan Martin, "There is grace this Holy Saturday," Facebook post, April 20, 2019, https://www.facebook.com/jonathan.martin.92167789/posts/1579427728868385.

Chapter 5 It's Good to Be a Fan

1. This is where Richard Rohr's language of "transcend and include" is so helpful. See, for example, Richard Rohr, *A Spring Within Us: A Book of Daily Meditations* (London: SPCK, 2016), 276–77.

2. I'm thinking of Jessica Walter's hilarious Lucille Bluth in *Arrested Development* shrieking whenever private detective Gene Parmesan shows up in a different guise. "Gene Parmesan . . . ahhhh!!!"

3. Since St. Paul will refer to him as the One who is "not far from each one of us . . . in [whom] we live and move and have our being" (Acts 17:27–28), there aren't some weird metaphysics involved in which everything hinges on whether or not you formally say the words that let him in. It is more about an intentional opening up to Love who has always been present for you, with you, and in you, a presence of Love not only longing to be discovered but also longing itself.

4. Rowan Williams, *Tokens of Trust: An Introduction to Christian Belief* (Louisville: Westminster John Knox, 2007), 21–22.

5. Marilynne Robinson, *Gilead* (New York: Farrar, Strauss & Giroux, 2004), 177.

Chapter 7 People of the Burning Heart

1. For the full context, read 2 Corinthians 3 from the Message translation.

2. The health of one's religion, incidentally, hinges largely on a handful of words: whether Jesus's "kingdom of heaven" simply means "going to heaven when you die" or God's peaceful, heavenly reign available to us on earth; whether language of fire and judgment looks like how God treats his enemies or how you would treat yours if you could; and whether "sin" is primarily understood as a way of violating an arbitrary moral code or violating your neighbor.

3. Jonathan Martin, "I Believe in Fire," Facebook post, January 18, 2017, https://www.facebook.com/jonathan.martin.92167789/posts/963658350445329.

4. You can hear my conversation with Rachel in a two-part *Zeitcast* that commemorated the one-year anniversary of her death. The portion I've quoted here is from "Conversations with Rachel Held Evans, Part 1," May 4, 2020, 31:47, http://jonathanmartinwords.com/the-zeitcast/2020/5/4/conversations-with-rachel-held-evans.

Chapter 9 What Had Happened on the Road

1. "Conversations with Rachel Held Evans, Part 1," 49:55.

Jonathan Martin is a writer, poet, and speaker who has undergone his own experience of finding God on the underside of life. Wherever he goes, his message is always the same: no matter who you are, where you've been, or what you've done, God is at work to bring beauty out of your brokenness. He has a ThM from Duke University and an MA from The Pentecostal Theological Seminary. Currently he lives in Oklahoma City, Oklahoma, where he serves as pastor of The Table and host of *The Zeitcast.*

CONNECT
WITH JONATHAN

jonathanmartinwords.com

Follow him on social media

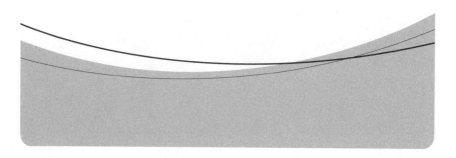